VINTAGE INNOVATION

LEVERAGING RETRO TOOLS AND CLASSIC IDEAS TO DESIGN DEEPER LEARNING EXPERIENCES

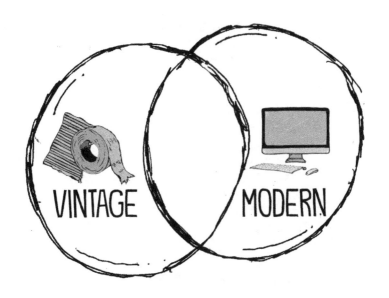

VINTAGE   MODERN

WRITTEN AND ILLUSTRATED BY
JOHN SPENCER

Vintage Innovation: Leveraging Retro Tools and Classic Ideas to Design Deeper Learning Experiences
Copyright © 2020 by John Spencer

BLEND
Blend Education
PO Box 5953
Salem, OR 97304

Paperback ISBN: 978-1-7341725-5-3
eBook ISBN: 978-1-7341725-6-0

CONTENTS

VINTAGE INNOVATION IS A BOTH / AND APPROACH

It's an embrace of the tried and true
and the never tried. It's a mash-up
of low-fi tech and new tech. It's the idea of finding
relevance by looking back and looking forward.
It's a focus on timeless skills in new contexts.
It's the idea that innovation happens when
teachers take a both/and approach as they
empower their students.

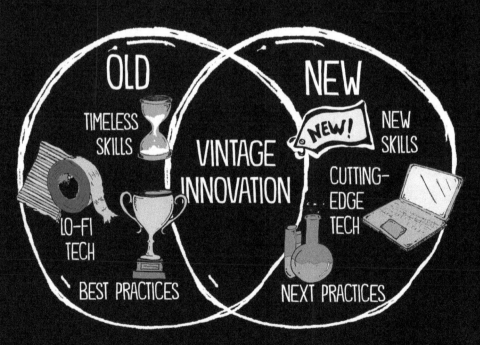

WHEN A TEACHER EMBRACES VINTAGE INNOVATION, THEY ASK . . .

- [ ] HOW DO I INNOVATE WHEN I DON'T HAVE THE BEST TECHNOLOGY?

- [ ] HOW CAN I USE VINTAGE TOOLS, IDEAS, AND APPROACHES IN NEW WAYS?

- [ ] HOW CAN I USE CONSTRAINTS TO SPARK CREATIVITY?

- [ ] HOW DO I BLEND TOGETHER THE TRIED AND TRUE WITH THE NEVER TRIED?

ACCESS THE FREE TOOLKIT

Note that this is a "big idea" book. It's about a mindset that we can have as educators. It's about an approach to innovation that runs counter to futurism.

This book is not an instruction manual. For what it's worth, I don't believe that teaching can be reduced down to a set of instructions or recipes or easy, sequential steps. It's a deeply personal journey filled with mistakes and bruised knees and failed experiments.

However, while I don't believe in recipes, I do believe we, as teachers, can always use tools and blueprints and exemplars that we can modify as we design projects for our students. For this reason, I have included a resources at the end of the chapter. I have put together these tools into a free toolkit that you can access at **vintageinnovationbook.com/toolkit.**

This toolkit will be an evolving set of resources. My goal is to send you updates every so often with new resources I have added.

CHAPTER 1

WE CAN'T PREDICT THE
FUTURE

My heart is hammering as I step toward the podium and approach the crowd gathered together at the White House. Pulse pounding and voice wavering, I begin my talk. The theme is "the future ready student." However, I begin with a confession. I don't know what students need for the future. I don't have a grand vision for how to transform schools. I can't predict the economy that my students will encounter or the world they will inhabit. My classroom isn't futuristic. We can't afford a 3D printer or a CAD machine. We don't have a state-of-the-art makerspace.

So, instead, I tell a story. Our story. The story of how my students explored an issue in their community and developed empathy with those in their neighborhoods and how they engaged in research and content curation as they studied the nuance and complexity of these issues. They used design thinking to develop unique, human-centered solutions. They blended together old school tools with newer technology.

The unit didn't go perfectly. Students hit roadblocks and some of them struggled to finish their projects. At one point, I got impatient and raised my voice. There were times that we, as a team of teachers, didn't provide our students with the right scaffolds. But despite my flaws as a teacher, I got to watch my students find their voice.

Now, years later, I get to watch my former students change the world. Alejandra, the once-shy student still learning English, is now a bold and brave teacher transforming learning at the same low-income school she once attended. Jesus and Sergio have taken voice and choice to the next level by co-creating and running Pride Apparel, an LGBT+ clothing line in New York City[1].

IF WE WANT TO PREPARE
STUDENTS FOR THE

FUTURE,

WE NEED TO EMPOWER
THEM IN THE

PRESENT.

As a teacher, I could never have predicted where my students would end up. I had no clue whether computer programming or theater or woodshop would end up as the most relevant subjects to their lives. I couldn't have predicted what apps or tools they would someday use. And yet, I've watched as those wild-eyed dreamers have stepped up to change their world in profound ways. Part of why this happened is because of the amazing teachers they had, like Javier and Crystal and Allison, who empowered them with voice and choice.

THE FUTURE HAS NEVER BEEN KNOWN

In 1984, psychologist and political scientist Philip E. Tetlock began a project to see how well expert researchers could predict the future. Over the next two decades, Tetlock gathered 82,361 probability estimates about the future. The end result was staggering. Expert researchers, with access to classified information and connections to powerful change-makers were dreadful at forecasting the future[2].

There was, however, a silver lining. Tetlock found a group of researchers who regularly outperformed their peers. These experts tended to be flexible thinkers and more open to new insights. They also had seemingly disconnected interests that they drew upon. He called these researchers "foxes" for their nimble, flexible approach. According to Tetlock, foxes "draw from an eclectic array of traditions, and accept ambiguity and contradiction."[3] He called the other group hedgehogs because they tended to stay burrowed down in their knowledge as experts in a single subject. In other words, if we want to know about the future, we need to ask, "What does the fox say?" That's right, I made a bad dad joke right there.

Six years later, the Intelligence Advanced Research Projects Activity launched a contest to see how well research teams could forecast the future. While most teams chose well-known experts, Tetlock and Barbara Mellers[4] created the Good Judgment Project. Instead of choosing experts, they asked for volunteers and chose a team from the 3,200 applicants. Here, they focused on people who had diverse interests and tended to read works in unrelated disciplines.

The Good Judgment Project team crushed the competition. So, what made this team different? First, they were intellectually humble. They knew that the future was unpredictable and thus they were more likely to seek out other opinions. Furthermore, they were divergent thinkers.[5]

Rather than viewing information as isolated and siloed, they made connections between ideas and disciplines. Finally, they were curious. One of the top team members described the team as "curious about, well, really everything."[6]

If this doesn't surprise you, it's because this curiosity is what we, as educators try to cultivate in our students. This is what happens every time teachers do projects and experiments and debates that inspire wonder and creativity in their students. While it might not seem like a big deal, these are the experiences that inspire students to become the innovators of the future.

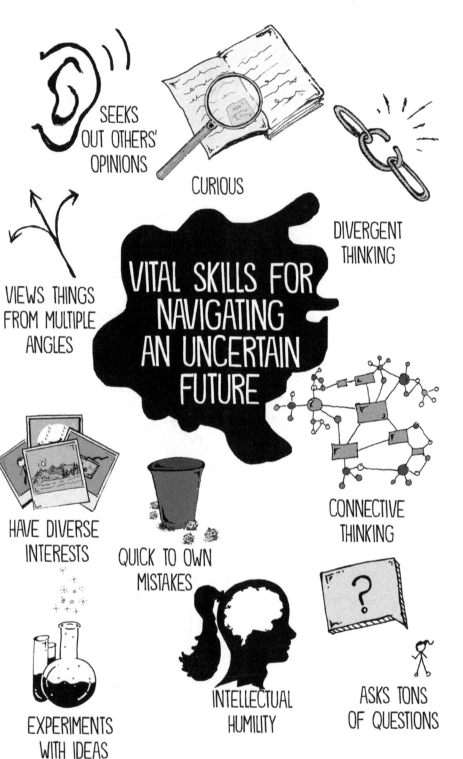

SEEKS OUT OTHERS' OPINIONS

CURIOUS

DIVERGENT THINKING

VIEWS THINGS FROM MULTIPLE ANGLES

VITAL SKILLS FOR NAVIGATING AN UNCERTAIN FUTURE

HAVE DIVERSE INTERESTS

QUICK TO OWN MISTAKES

CONNECTIVE THINKING

EXPERIMENTS WITH IDEAS

INTELLECTUAL HUMILITY

ASKS TONS OF QUESTIONS

THE GOLDEN DISC PROMISE

When I was in the seventh grade, one of my teachers called the entire class up to the front of the room. He held up a shiny golden disc in wild excitement.

"This will change education forever," he said, eyes gleaming. "Someday, you'll be able to pick up one of these discs and learn exactly what you need to learn. No more taking notes from a teacher. You won't have to learn from someone like me."

I felt uneasy about learning from a golden disc instead of a human. I liked my teacher. I liked how he would change his explanations on the spot just by reading our body language. I liked the way he made us laugh. I enjoyed the inefficient way he got off topic and we randomly learned things that weren't in the textbook. Why would I want to replace him with a golden disc?

"This is the future of education, kids," he said with a grin. "This will change things forever."

But it did not change education forever. I haven't seen a laser disc in three decades and I feel pretty confident that my own kids' teachers will not be replaced by golden discs. Not now. Not ever.

And yet, this is the same sentiment I have seen in many iterations. I've watched as one-to-one devices, laptops, and adaptive learning programs[78] have all promised to replace teachers. In a few years, it'll be A.I. Just get a Siri-styled assistant who can answer every student question with absolute precision without the messy mistakes that a teacher might make. However, I don't buy it.

Teaching will always be a deeply relational endeavor filled with mistakes and missteps and false starts. That's the beauty of it.

SO, IT TURNS OUT A

BOOK

IS ACTUALLY
THE PERFECT MOBILE DEVICE

One of the most powerful elements of the Social Voice Project – a citizen journalism project I launched in my second year of teaching – happened when I messed up and said, "I am sorry I yelled at our class. "The students responded with kindness and grace. However, algorithms can't be humble or human and they can't teach the kinds of lessons students learn we, as teachers, own our mistakes.

Nobody writes thank you notes to worksheets or adaptive learning platforms or AI machines. However, they will go to great lengths to find that one teacher who changed their life forever – despite that teacher's human imperfections.

As I look back at the laser disc moment of my childhood, I am reminded of how easy it is to mistake novelty for innovation. I'm not immune to this. I have an e-reader that gathers dust because it turns out a book is the perfect mobile device for distraction-free reading.

It's easy to choose futurism over innovation and forget just how clueless we humans are about the future. As teachers, we can't predict what Artificial Intelligence will look like in the upcoming decade. We can't predict what new disruptive technologies will change our world. But we do know that our students will need to be foxes rather than hedgehogs and as teachers, we can craft the learning experiences that empower students to become those foxes.

Our students will need to be flexible and nimble. They will need to be divergent thinkers and collaborators. They will need to be nimble. This book explores what it means to face the uncertainty of the future with a vintage innovation mindset.

CHAPTER 2

VINTAGE

FUTURE

THE FUTURE IS
VINTAGE

I meander the hallways, dodging chunks of cardboard and maneuvering through the maze of makeshift work stations. It's a two-day maker project where each team has to design a functioning pinball machine using limited materials. Snaking my way through the cacophony of high fives and cheers and frustrated grunts, I stare out at the students sprawled around the hallways.

Then I see it. A boy is using a saw to cut plastic. "Wait, where did you get that?"

"I made it," he answers.

"But you're supposed to use the supplies in the box," I point out.

"This was in our box," he pointed out. "Well, the raw material was in our box. See, we bent the metal in half to make it stronger and duct taped the plastic to the edges and now it works pretty well. Want to try it?"

I give it a whirl and it's surprisingly sturdy. This group has just transformed flimsy aluminum into a functioning saw. Another group is testing out ways to create the spring-loaded effect you typically get with the plunger (that rod used to shoot the pinball down the chute).

Downstairs, a team of freshmen work on another maker challenge. Right now, they're analyzing a survey for the types of sports kids like to play.

"I want us to make this truly inclusive. The directions tell us that this is a sport that anyone can play. Can we interview people who are blind or have limited mobility? I'm just thinking that if we really wanted kids to play this, we would want *all* kids to play this."

Another student adds, "I feel like the game should be intuitive because we have kids who might not speak English." She then shares what it was like for her to arrive to school as an immigrant, feeling terrified of learning a new language and navigating a new culture. "But then I played soccer at recess. That was my shared language. I could speak through movement. And I want to create that experience for other kids."

On the surface, these design projects seem almost childish for high school students. They're making pinball machines with items we would typically toss in the recycling bin and creating new sports using items like marbles, balloons, duct tape, and cardboard.

The faculty is taking a huge risk today with this maker project. Several seniors have taken the day off to work on their college admissions essays; viewing the project as "too easy" and not worth their time. Many of the students are baffled by the lack of resources. After all, they have a state-of-the-art makerspace that's going unused for the day. Within the first hour of the design challenge, a few students are openly questioning the relevance of the maker challenges.

"What does this have to do with our future?" a student asks.

"Everything," his teacher answers.

The student isn't happy with the one-word response, but his teacher is onto something. By limiting the supplies, the teachers are encouraging students to engage in divergent thinking. They are pushed to innovate, not in spite of the lack of fancy gadgetry, but because of the limited technology. These constraints also force students to iterate and improvise.

But I also notice something else at work: struggle. At one group, a student walks away and throws her hands up in frustration. "I just . . . can't . . . I mean, it won't work. Why won't it work?"

Tears stream down her cheeks. When I ask her what's wrong, she says, "I'm supposed to be good at this stuff. I'm going to be a science major. I should know this. I passed the AP Physics test. I'm a good student."

Twenty minutes later, I hear an audible cheer. This same girl who walked away in frustration is now pushing through and solving the problem. Her tear-stained face is now beaming. It's just a pinball machine but it's also so much more.

This project is forcing students to work through iterations slowly with tons of mistakes. Although they get frustrated, the students are also fully engaged in deep and meaningful work. Slowly, students who had called in absent start trickling in after receiving text messages from their teammates admitting that it's actually pretty fun.

By the end of the day, the hallway is buzzing with excitement. One team is exchanging phone numbers so that they can meet up and figure out a better way to design the flippers on their pinball machine. They're choosing to do homework. For fun. Let that sink in for a moment. If that's not a near-miracle, I don't know what is.

Throughout these two days, I watch the teachers facilitate student collaboration, problem-solving, and creativity. A few students who viewed this mini-project as childish become passionate about what they are creating.

This is a small example of vintage innovation. It's an overlap between the old and the new.

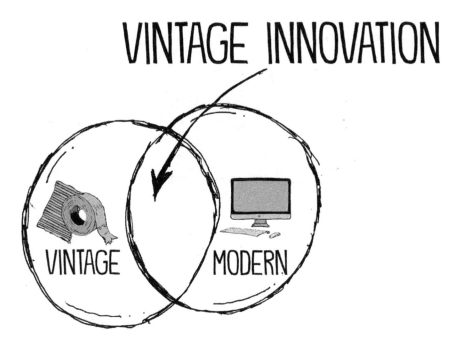

For example, students film videos to share both their journey and their finished product with the world. They engage in research online. A few students do a quick video conference with an expert engineer. But it's also deeply vintage. Students engage in prototyping using duct tape and cardboard rather than just a 3D printer. They mash-up old ideas in fresh ways. They embrace creative constraint.

The most powerful element in this project is the human connection that happens when students collaborate and create and solve problems together. True, it's just a pinball machine or a sport with plastic cups and marbles. But it's also so much more. It's collaboration and empathy and problem-solving and creativity.

OUR WORLD IS CHANGING

When I was a kid, this bad boy was considered cutting-edge.

The biggest technology concern I had was avoiding dysentery while making it to western Oregon.

Times have changed. The device I carry around in my pocket is more powerful than what I could have imagined as a kid.

NOW

THEN

MY KIDS WILL NEVER KNOW
THE STRUGGLE OF SPENDING
HOURS TRYING TO MAKE A

MIX TAPE

If you look at your phone, there's an entire suite of apps that used to exist only in the physical world: a compass, a calculator, maps, video cameras, cameras, and mail.

My kids will never know the struggle of standing in front of your boom box with the finger on the record button, just waiting for that Nirvana song to come on so that you could have an epic mix tape. (Just kidding. It was totally Boys II Men.) Now kids just say, "Hey Alexa, play my favorite song" and it happens.

My kids will never know what it's like to get purple Ditto ink off your hands when you had filled out a worksheet. They'll never need to navigate dark magic of the microfiche machine to look up an old article. Now, they type away on Chromebooks and find articles up in seconds.

My kids will never have to avoid getting clotheslined by the 90-foot long phone cord in the kitchen as your mom was chatting with the neighbor while you perfect a *Matrix*-like acrobatic stance just to get a drink of water. They'll never have to worry about saving something to a disk and then, hours later, hoping it wasn't all erased because it was too close to a magnet. They'll never know a world where their devices didn't talk back them and where computers weren't touchscreens. They'll never have to fix a broken cassette with the top of a pencil or unjam a slide projector or pick up the phone and listen to make sure no one was talking on it before trying to get online only to wait five painfully long minutes for the dial-up to work.

This generation will never have to blow on a video game cartridge to see if that magically makes it work, even though that's been scientifically proven not to work[9]. They'll never have to wait by the mailbox for a letter to arrive or time a long-distance phone call for the cheapest time of the week. They'll never know what it's like to work on an essay at the last minute only to have to change the ribbon on the typewriter or wait for the whiteout to dry. They'll never have to wait days for camera film to develop.

And yet, this is just the beginning. The prevalence of social media means our students will grow up with a worldview shaped by algorithms[10] as much as families or neighborhoods. Meanwhile, robotics and automation continue to replace manufacturing jobs.[11] Rapid prototyping is now easier than ever and we're just beginning to see what can happen with automation and machine learning.[12] Virtual reality is still in its infancy and we can't predict what it will mean for the way we perceive our world. Moreover, our students will enter a world where artificial intelligence will replace a significant number of analytical jobs.[13]

In the face of these rapid changes, it's easy to think, "Let's prepare them for the future. Let's transform our schools into places that are cutting edge and new." Maybe add some high-tech makerspaces and launch coding classes. Let's teach students how to use the 3D printer. Let's teach them how to use Augmented Reality and Virtual Reality. Let's teach every child to master coding.

But here's the counterintuitive truth: if we want to prepare our students for this future, we shouldn't focus on the solely future. As a teacher, I've seen the promise of interactive whiteboards, personalized learning programs, and one-to-one netbooks to revolutionize education. Years later, many of these gadgets are now obsolete.

But certain strategies will never be obsolete. Deep conversations. Meaningful collaboration. Epic projects. Creative thinking. Curiosity. These are the strategies that will help students become adaptable, nimble, and able to iterate. If they can think divergently and make connections between unrelated ideas, they'll actually anticipate change more quickly.

In other words, instead of focusing on distinctly 21st Century Skills, we should focus on timeless skills. We often hear about 21st Century Skills[14] like collaboration, problem-solving, communication, and creativity. However, these aren't 21st Century Skills. They have always been vital to life and they will remain vital in the future.

SOFT SKILLS HAVE ALWAYS MATTERED

For years, Google focused on recruiting the best computer science students who excelled in their studies. They assumed that innovation required the students from the best universities. But when they tested this hypothesis with their Project Oxygen report (an inventory of what factors were the best predictors of employee success), they were shocked by the results. The top skills were the "soft skills," like being a problem-solver, being teachable, communicating effectively, having empathy, and making connections between seemingly unrelated ideas.[15] Notice that these aren't 21st Century Skills. They're timeless skills. They're the skills hunter-gatherers needed and the skills we'll need in 300 years.

Instead of focusing on technology skills to compete with Artificial Intelligence or automation, students should develop soft skills. They need to develop deeply human mindsets and habits that will set them apart. This begins with the question, "What can humans do that machines can't do?"

The answer is oddly vintage. Artificial intelligence is amazing in its ability to determine patterns and follow algorithms, which is why students will need to take a more vintage approach and think divergently to solve complex problems in unique ways. Engineers will use 3D printing to make amazing products, but the best design will always start with empathy and is often inspired by studying nature. Moreover, some of the best creative approaches borrow from older disciplines. Later in this book, I'll share the example of how an ancient artform is reshaping the future of space travel.

Surrounded by a sea of information, students will need to learn the vintage art of curation. In a globalized world, students will need to embrace the local. With augmented reality and virtual reality at their fingertips, students will need to engage in play and imagination and curiosity. In other words, to be more relevant, they will need to be different.

FLASHY AND NEW ➜ BETTER AND DIFFERENT

This idea is at the heart of vintage innovation: if we want students to become innovators, we need to choose "better and different" rather than "flashy and new."

TEACHERS ARE AT THE HEART OF INNOVATION

Authentic, long-lasting innovation can't be found in a new app or a set of slick gadgets or a new system. All of these things are necessary, but they will ultimately grow obsolete. The tools and systems will always remain secondary to the greatest influence of innovation: the teacher. Think about your most epic project you did as a student. No doubt, most of the technology is now obsolete. You might have even forgotten the tools you used or the programs you learned. But you'll never forget that teacher.

When teachers embrace vintage innovation, they design learning experiences that last forever. They look forward by looking back. They mash-up old-school analog tools with new tools and strategies. They look at challenges as opportunities and incorporate barriers into design solutions. This doesn't mean they ignore injustice or accept the status quo. Instead, they actively work to transform spaces for all learners. But these teachers also don't allow constraints to be an excuse for complacency. Instead, they see constraints as chances to innovate.

My good friend Javier Lucero embodies this vintage innovation approach. Javi and I spent years working together in the same urban, low-income school in Phoenix, Arizona. Sometimes we would get frustrated by the fact that we couldn't get fancier equipment. We would lament the uptight policies of a rigid school system that emphasized standardized test scores. However, every time we vented our frustrations, he would say, "So, how are we going to solve this problem?"

Javi's favorite question was "Why not?" When we couldn't get computers for our classroom, he asked "why not? What are we missing?" Months later, when our librarian and principal were lamenting about the old computers on the ground, I commented, "Well, no computer is too old if the hardware still works. You just run them on Linux and they'll be fine. I bet someone would want them."

Javi responded with, "Someone? How about us? We want them."

A month later, we were converting these broken-down machines into faster, open source Linux computers. We not only found a new use for these old tools, but we integrated the emerging digital world with the hands-on physical world to create a social studies class that incorporated a vintage innovation approach of digital journalism, service learning, and philosophy.

Another time, when the district had low attendance for an intervention-based summer school, he asked, "Why can't we just make it a STEM camp instead?" He transformed a bland, traditional desks-in-rows summer school into an active, human-oriented summer camp that students would beg to enter. It was a true vintage innovation space that combined gardening with robotics with digital journalism and cardboard prototyping. Over a decade later, he still gets emails from former students thanking him for the skills they learned in that camp. To Javi, it wasn't a big deal. It's what he did. But it was a big deal to his students.

Javi's innovative solutions inspired hundreds of future artists and engineers and makers. But Javi's not alone. There are countless educators choosing the vintage innovation route of "different and better" rather than "flashy and new." Many of these teachers work in buildings that don't have the fanciest makerspaces. Their students might not have access to 3D printers or CAD machines. However, these teachers work within these constraints to design innovative learning experiences every single day.

Technology skills will continue to change. But there are these things that are timeless – creativity, collaboration, critical thinking, divergent thinking, empathy, project management, endurance, flexibility – and they are the very thing that computers can't do well. These are the skills that teachers instill in their students when they design epic projects and embrace a mindset of vintage innovation.

For the last two years, I have traveled to different schools listening to the innovative stories of teachers. As a full-time professor, I have been in classrooms watching teachers embrace this idea of vintage innovation as well. It has been a reminder that countless teachers are doing amazing things. Similarly, when I was doing research for this book, I sent out a survey to my blog readers and had over 300 teachers respond with their inspiring stories of vintage innovation. The response was so overwhelming, I couldn't even interview most of them.

In this book, I share stories from my own experiences as a middle school teacher along with stories about the amazing teachers I worked with at the time. I also share stories from the teachers I've observed as a professor and the amazing teachers I've met through blogging and social media. My first hope is that you will not only feel inspired to try something new but also affirmed for the innovative work you're already doing. My second hope is that you finish this book with at least one innovative idea you plan to implement.

Gadgets will come and go. However, one thing will always remain: the impact you have on your students' lives when you empower them with voice and choice. You will always be at the heart of innovation.

CHAPTER 3

WHAT IS VINTAGE INNOVATION?

The Astrodome was a modern miracle, a Space Age wonder, with a glass dome, high-tech air-conditioning, and the world's biggest scoreboard.[16] When it opened in 1965, reporters dubbed it the "8th Wonder of the World."[17] This was the pinnacle of innovation. No more bad weather or quirky dimensions or any other pesky variables that made baseball messy and unpredictable. With the largest Jumbotron, the trendiest color choices (orange and yellow) and a modern symmetrical design, it embodied the Space Age.

This was the ballpark of the future.

Until the first game.

Within minutes of the first pitch, people noticed a fatal flaw. Seasoned outfielders couldn't catch a simple fly ball. It turns out it's hard to see a high-speed baseball when you're staring into the glare of giant windows. Simple solution. Just paint the ceiling tiles glass. But this, in turn, killed the grass, which led to the patented Astro Turf, a smooth, clean-looking, easy to manage artificial turf that added to the futuristic feel of the stadium. If you grew up in the 80's, you probably remember the mint green carpet in over half of all the baseball stadiums. Unfortunately, this initial version of Astro Turf led to career-ending injuries for the players.[18]

See, the Astrodome wasn't designed for the players. It was future-focused, not player-focused or fan-focused or even baseball-focused. Within two decades, this "8th Wonder of the World" became a concrete relic of the false promise of futurism. The design team had defined innovation as future-driven rather than purpose-driven. In the process, they created something flashy and novel rather than timeless and innovative.

By the mid-1980's, nearly every Major League Baseball team had built their own massive modern stadium. But these multipurpose stadiums were a disaster for fans. With bland aesthetics, horrible sight lines, and way too many seats, these concrete donuts were concrete disappointments. But then everything changed in the late 1980's with a bold new idea: Go vintage. Find inspiration in the ideas they had abandoned in the Astrodome Era. Oriole Park in Camden Yards would be quirky, creative, and connected to the community. It would be fan-focused rather than future-focused.

THE ASTRODOME	CAMDEN YARDS
Futuristic	Timeless
Isolated	Connected to community
Blank Slate	Creative constraint
Focused on Innovation	Focused on the Players and Fans

When the team's owner pushed for a multi-purpose stadium, the team president, Larry Lucchino, pushed back. "Let's look at the most successful baseball franchises out there. The Yankees in Yankee Stadium. The Cubs in Wrigley Field. The Red Sox in Fenway Park. And what did they have in common? They all played in a baseball-only facility, a facility that was designed for baseball and did not compromise architecturally for other sports."[19]

The architectural team chose to look backward to look forward. Their vision was a "an old-fashioned traditional baseball park with modern amenities." They borrowed ideas from Ebbets Field, Shibe Park, the Polo Grounds, and other ballparks that had been demolished and replaced with concrete donuts.

Instead of building with a clean slate at the edge of the suburbs, they designed the ballpark in the heart of the city. Rather than bulldozing the enormous old B&O warehouse, they incorporated it into the design[20]. Similarly, the oddly-shaped plot of land contributed to the quirky field dimensions and unique sightlines. In other words, they embraced limitations and treated barriers as design features.

In the end, they built a cozy ballpark with a view of the city skyline and an atmosphere that felt timeless. Decades later, Camden Yards has already lasted longer than the Astrodome. It's still relevant. Camden Yards was a case of vintage innovation – incorporating old ideas and approaches into a new design in a way proves timeless rather than novel.

SOMETIMES THE BEST WAY TO MOVE **BOLDLY** INTO THE FUTURE IS TO EXPLORE THE IDEAS OF THE PAST

WHAT IS VINTAGE INNOVATION?

Vintage innovation is the overlap of old ideas and strategies, with new technology, contexts, and knowledge. It's the idea of an "old-fashioned baseball park with modern amenities." It's what happens when we use classic ideas to solve current problems but it's also what happens when we use conventional materials in fresh ways.

Note that vintage innovation isn't a nostalgic call to go back to the "good old days." The past is full of examples of hatred, bigotry, racism, and slavery. Massive wars. Rampant misogyny. We want students to examine history with a critical eye rather than rose-colored glasses.

Furthermore, vintage innovation is not a fear-based rejection of new tools or new ideas. It's not a blanket statement that smart phones have ruined community or a curmudgeonly complaint about "kids these days who play video games all the time." We don't need to throw our laptops into the dumpster or move into a yurt in the forest.

Vintage innovation actually includes an embrace of technology. As a classroom teacher, I used VR headsets to take students on expeditions. But the goal wasn't "let's learn how to use the tech." Instead, it was, "let's go see something fascinating." My goal is not to teach students to "learn how to blog," but I love blogging for the way it allows students to express their voice and share their work with the audience. I used to spend weeks teaching students how to code. However, my goal was never to develop future coders. It was to help them learn logic and strategy. They could have learned these same skills playing Chess.

Vintage innovation is intentionally both/and. It's about finding the overlap between analog and digital. It's about building the bridge between the past and the future. Like all innovation, vintage innovation is inherently disruptive. But it's disruptive by pulling us out of present tense and into something more timeless and sustainable.

It can help to think of vintage innovation with a chart of what is and what it is not:

WHAT IT IS	WHAT IT ISN'T
Both/And	Either/Or
Using tech wisely (including old tools)	Avoiding technology at all costs
Thinking critically about past	Nostalgically embracing the past
Fighting against injustice	Ignoring injustice
Embracing sustainable change	Fighting against change

BIG IDEA #1
VINTAGE TOOLS OFTEN FORCE US TO INNOVATE

I remember feeling frustrated as a teacher in a Title One school. We didn't have a fancy makerspace or a fab lab or a high-tech studio. I would visit schools or look at slideshows in conferences and think, "Man, if I had better tools, I could totally pull off innovative projects." Later, I realized something. These limitations often forced me to innovate in my classroom. They weren't merely barriers I had to work around. They were often the very design features I used to create meaningful projects.

In my twelve years in the classroom, we never once had access to a 3D printer. I remember feeling like we weren't doing "real" maker projects. However, my students were designing amazing products using duct tape and cardboard – because of the creative constraints of having fewer tools.[21]

Vintage tools force us to think creatively. The lack of options push students to tap into their internal creativity rather than accessing pre-programmed templates. For example, I first got into whiteboard videos when I realized that we would never have the money for state-of-the-art studio equipment. And yet, those sketch videos were highly creative because of the limitations of the medium. Similarly, when we didn't have the money or the high-tech gadgetry to solve our campus graffiti problem, students came up with an innovative solution based on vintage tools – we would paint murals that nobody would want to tag up.

The bottom line is that vintage tools aren't merely the back-up plan when you don't have the money to purchase better equipment. Instead, they are often what lead to creative constraint and ultimately innovation.

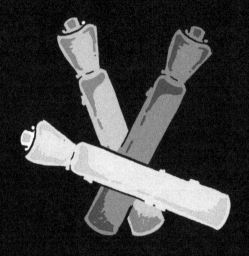

IN TEN YEARS,
MOST OF YOUR CLASSROOM
TECHNOLOGY WILL
BE PRETTY MUCH OBSOLETE,
BUT STUDENTS WILL STILL FIND
JOY IN SMELLY MARKERS

BIG IDEA #2
VINTAGE IDEAS INSPIRE POSSIBILITIES

Innovation isn't about being up-to-date with the newest gadgets and apps. It's about solving relevant problems in original ways. Instead of asking "what is new?" you ask, "what is best?" Sometimes the answer vintage. Sometimes the answer is something new. Often, it's a mash-up of the two.

Some of the most innovative ideas aren't new. Take project-based learning. It might seem like a buzzword. However, John Dewey advocated for "learning by doing"[22] in 1897 and by 1918 Kilpatrick introduced an early framework for project-based learning.[23] Our technology makes it easier than ever to connect to new information and craft products. But the idea is over a century old. Design thinking has its roots in the 1950's and 1960's.[24] And Socratic discussions go back to . . . well . . . antiquity. So, millennia. These ideas are innovative, not because they are new, but because they prepare students for a future where they will need to be self-directed and creative.

While these ideas and strategies have always been timely, they are actually more relevant than ever given the pace of change in our modern world.

BIG IDEA #3
VINTAGE INNOVATION FOCUSES ON THE TIMELESS

A decade ago, I watched a local school district purchase hundreds of interactive whiteboards. Hailed as the ultimate solution for student achievement,[25] teachers attended flip chart trainings. The school district purchased packaged curriculum promising huge results. Specialists observed classrooms to see if teachers were implementing the interactive whiteboards with fidelity. Now, many of those interactive whiteboards are being torn out and classrooms are re-installing physical whiteboards because dry erase markers are fast, efficient, and flexible.

Interactive whiteboards won't change learning. Tablets won't change learning. Virtual reality headsets won't change learning. It's about the role of the teacher as the designer of learning experiences. Always has been. Always will be.

I still remember one of the most life-changing learning experiences of my childhood. When I was in middle school, I spent an entire year working on a National History Day Project. It was the first time I had ever experienced true project-based learning. Throughout the entire school year, I worked on a single research project, taking a deep dive into the integration of baseball with Jackie Robinson. In the end, I entered the National History Day competition and shared my work with a larger audience.

Mrs. Smoot and Mr. Darrow inspired me to work harder than I had ever worked before by empowering me to own the process. I generated a list of questions, spent days in the library researching those questions, and ultimately interviewed former Negro League baseball players. I felt like a detective and a historian and a documentarian all at the same time.

It was exciting but also terrifying. I would script out my questions in advance and then nervously dial the numbers. Half the time, I would hang up. The other half, I would whisper, "This is John from Alta Sierra Middle School." Looking back on it, I'm sure these former players probably thought, "Holy crap, someone's whisper talking to me. I'm going to die." At least that's how it happens in the movies. These moments were eye-opening for me because many of the players described the challenges that occurred with the end of the Negro Leagues and the lack of black-owned baseball teams. I wasn't just learning how to communicate. I was learning empathy and I was gaining a new perspective on life.

Later, I wrote out a script and typed it out, word for word, on our trusty Smith-Corona, before examining it, line-by-line before my next draft. The process was slow and laborious but I didn't care. I was passionate about this topic and I wanted the world to see how the integration of baseball connected directly to the Civil Rights movement.

Eventually, I recorded my script and created an entire set of slides and presented it to my classmates and later to the district, state, and national competitions.

As I look back on this project, I can see that there were technology skills I learned and there were thinking skills that I also acquired.

TECHNOLOGY SKILLS	THINKING SKILLS
How to fix a jammed slide projector	How to solve problems
How to take a picture and develop the film into a slide	How to tell a story visually
How to find articles on microfiche	How to read with a critical eye and curate sources
How to make long-distance phone calls	How to conduct interviews
How to splice together audio using a razor blade and Scotch tape	How to communicate clearly and professionally even when you're terrified
How to use dial-up Internet	How to connect with a global audience
How to change a ribbon on a typewriter	How share my voice with the world

I no longer need any of those skills on the left side of the list. As an eighth-grader, I had to splice together audio by using a razor blade and Scotch tape to edit the magnetic reels. Now, I easily edit multiple audio tracks on my computer. I created slides by painstakingly adjusting the lighting, snapping a photograph and developing the film at a drug store. Now, I edit photos quickly on Photoshop and arrange animated slideshows on Keynote or PowerPoint. I used to write to experts through the mail. Now, I can do a video-conference anywhere at any time.

Meanwhile, I regularly use the skills on the right side of the list. These are the timeless, transferrable skills that will never grow obsolete. This doesn't mean we ignore technology skills. I'm glad, for example, that I learned how to type and how to create a spreadsheet in middle school. However, when we choose our tools, we should focus on how our tool selection will help develop the skills on the right side of the list.

Focusing on the future nearly always leads to futurism. However, vintage innovation recognizes that the future is unpredictable and therefore we should focus on timeless skills.

However, this all begins with teachers. Mrs. Smoot and Mr. Darrow empowered me with voice and choice and ownership. Rather than diving into the "tech-based learning," they focused on timeless skills and taught me to blend together the old and the new.

THE MOST INNOVATIVE TEACHER I KNOW

I know of this amazing teacher. We'll call Phyllis (since that's her name). Phyllis Mowery-Racz is a master innovator but if you asked her about it, she'd laugh at the word "innovation." She'd tell you that it took her forever to learn how to use a smart phone and she'd point to ten other teachers who are more techie than her. But don't let that fool you. She spent over thirty years sparking creativity and developing a maker mindset in her students.

As an art teacher, Phyllis empowered her students with voice and choice. She would mash-up old concepts with new art movements. Every summer she would seek out new instructional strategies and combine them with the tried and true strategies she had developed for years. Her students learned to embrace the digital and the analog in projects that mashed-up lo-fi materials with cutting edge technology – like their steam punk insect project, where they upcycled materials to create mechanical bugs. For Phyllis, each project was an experiment and she was fearless about pushing the envelope.

After over thirty years in the classroom, Phyllis retired . . . for a summer. Then she came back and taught computers and STEM with the same fearless determination. She learned to code so that her students could learn to code. She learned to blog so that her students could learn to blog. She studied Photoshop techniques, so she could teach it within a photojournalism project. For the next four years, she honed her craft, taking bold experiments – some of which failed.

Phyllis would be the first to tell you she wasn't a tech geek. But that didn't matter. She was innovative. She was always trying new approaches and layering next practices onto best practices. And yet, her goal was never innovation. It was always about the students. How could she empower them to be more creative? How could she create a climate where they would take creative risks? What would it mean to maximize collaboration while respecting each student's voice?

Phyllis is now retired – for real this time (okay, we'll see). However, she discovered something profound early on in her career: that innovation is the means to an end. Her real focus was always her students not on trying to be more innovative. Earlier in this chapter, I mentioned that Camden Yards focused on the players and the fans rather than the future. Vintage innovation was the design method but not the design goal. Similarly, Phyllis used vintage innovation as a method for her ultimate goal of student voice and choice. By empowering them in the present, she prepared them to become the divergent thinkers, curators, and makers that are shaping our future.

Like Phyllis, when we embody a vintage innovation mindset, we focus on our students rather than focusing on the future.

CHAPTER 4

IN A WORLD OF CONSTANT CHANGE, OUR STUDENTS NEED TO BE

DIVERGENT THINKERS

When I was a kid, my twin brother and I loved watching *American Gladiators*. You remember, Lace, Zap, Blaze, Ice, and all the other characters whose names either sounded like dangerous street drugs or onomatopoeia? Over time, we became more and more inspired to create our own *American Gladiators* show in our backyard. We spent a whole day sketching out our plans for how we would turn this dream into a reality.

Unfortunately, we didn't have the wood, pipes, and padding we needed to make a true gladiator course. We did, however, have two baseball bats, some old puffy slippers, and duct tape. These limited supplies proved to be perfect for recreating the jousting gam e. Next, we discussed the ideal location for building a platform. Initially, we thought we'd set it up on the swing set and then build a foam pit underneath. Sadly, we didn't have foam and our dad wouldn't let us dig a giant pit. So, we jotted down ideas until we finally landed on the idea of the bunk bed. We stacked the two box springs and mattresses on the floor and stood on the top bunk of our shared bunkbed. We hung our own hand-painted *American Gladiators* sign, donned our red, white, and blue costumes and created our gladiator names. Mine was Tang (as in the orange drink astronauts used in space). It wasn't a very good Gladiator name. Then again, I wasn't a very good Gladiator. Every time I won, I would apologize – which I suppose would make me more like a Canadian Gladiator than an American Gladiator.

Still, the project was epic.

We spent hours playing our game, adding slight variations on it and eventually hacking the rules to make it less and less like *American Gladiators* and more and more like *The Spencer Twin Gladiators*. Looking back on it, I'm not sure if we ever asked permission. I'm not even sure if my parents knew what we were doing. These were the pre-helicopter parenting days.

Although we didn't realize it at the time, something powerful was happening when we invented our *American Gladiators* game.

We were developing divergent thinking skills. It's the same thing that happened when we grabbed whatever random household objects we could find to design new musical instruments. In both cases, we started with a bold idea and a lack of supplies. However, this creative constraint pushed us to "hack" the objects around us until we solved the problem and created something original. At the time, it wasn't a big deal. We were just playing. However, this play cultivated the very divergent thinking that my brother and I both use as adults. My brother works in finance and I'm a professor. However, we both face frequent situations where we need to find unique solutions to complex problems.

We can think divergently because we spent our childhood hacking together solutions with the resources we had. Apparently, that's what happens when you try to be an American Gladiator.

Imagine you have a problem you need to solve and you're looking for innovative solutions. In this moment, there's a good chance you'll choose one of two cognitive approaches. In 1956, the psychologist J.P. Guilford coined the terms convergent thinking and divergent thinking to describe these contrasting approaches[26]. Convergent thinking is linear and systematic while divergent thinking is web-like, focusing on the connections between ideas. Convergent thinking narrows down multiple ideas into a single solution.

THEY THINK
OUTSIDE THE BOX

THEY ARE
PREPARED FOR
THE CREATIVE
ECONOMY

THEY BECOME
PROBLEM-SOLVERS

THEY BECOME
SYSTEMS THINKERS

THEY USE
MATERIALS
IN UNUSUAL
WAYS

WHEN STUDENTS BECOME
**DIVERGENT
THINKERS**

THEY TAKE
CREATIVE RISKS

THEY EXPERIMENT
WITH NEW IDEAS

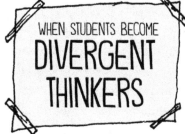

THEY ENGAGE
IN ITERATIVE
THINKING

THEY BECOME
WILDLY AND UNABSHEDLY
DIFFERENT

THEY LEARN TO WORK
WITHIN CREATIVE
CONSTRAINTS

THEY LEARN TO
NAVIGATE
CHALLENGES

48

On the other hand, divergent thinking expands outward by generating multiple ideas, often thinking like a hacker and using materials in original ways. Here, you treat barriers as design opportunities. Convergent thinking tends to be more focused while divergent thinking is more flexible and iterative. Convergent thinking is analytical and focused on what's best. By contrast, divergent thinking is open-ended. Participants are encouraged to take creative risks. even though some ideas might not work. Convergent thinking asks, "Why?" Divergent thinking asks, "Why not?"

CONVERGENT THINKING	DIVERGENT THINKING
Narrows down	Expands out
Focused	Flexible
Why?	Why not?
Analytical	Imaginative

While these might seem like competitive approaches, they actually go hand-in-hand[27]. Often, teams will use divergent thinking to generate multiple ideas followed by convergent thinking to analyze and narrow down ideas. Later, they might use divergent thinking to come up with fresh perspectives, followed by convergent thinking, in an ongoing cycle.

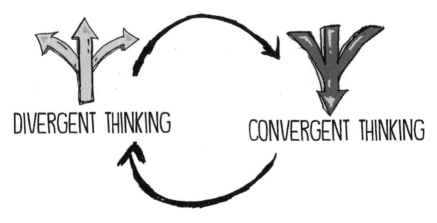

DIVERGENT THINKING   CONVERGENT THINKING

Unfortunately, the standardized approach to school works against divergent thinking by emphasizing convergent thinking alone[28]. In the United States, our current climate emphasizes achievement scores on high-stakes tests impacting everything from teacher evaluations to school report card grades. Instead of jumping back and forth between disciplines, the standardized approach encourages students to focus on each of the core subjects separately. The system rewards students for getting the right answer without asking "can you find a different answer?"

However, as we think of the future, our students will need to be divergent thinkers. Our students will enter a tumultuous global economy as automation and artificial intelligence continue to replace analytical jobs. Our students will need to be nimble. They will need to know how to experiment, iterate, and pivot. This is where divergent thinking becomes so critical. Divergent thinkers make connections between seemingly random ideas. In the process, they find innovative solutions by looking at things from different angles, often finding inspiration from surprising contexts. Here, students learn how to "hack" items by using them in unexpected ways. They figure out how to mash-up two seemingly unrelated ideas. This is the type of thinking that can't be techsourced. While artificial intelligence focuses on patterns and sequential processes, divergent thinking steps away from the algorithm to generate something that is both original and practical.

SCHOOLS OFTEN FOCUS
ON GETTING THE
RIGHT ANSWER . . .

. , . AND GETTING
IT QUICKLY.

HOWEVER, DIVERGENT THINKING
IS ABOUT FINDING
A DIFFERENT APPROACH,
EVEN IF IT TAKES LONGER.

And yet, divergent thinking is inherently vintage. After all, divergent thinkers have been changing the world for centuries. Consider the printing press. It was essentially a mash-up of a wine-press and a die/punch[29]. In the 1830's, Edwin Budding used carding tools (the technology for trimming textiles) to create the first lawnmower[30] More recently, Sir James Dyson revolutionized vacuums by applying the cyclonic separation technology from sawmills into his vacuum cleaner design.[31] With divergent thinking, you apply ideas and approaches from one domain into a seemingly unrelated context resulting in creative solutions.

FIVE DIVERGENT THINKING STRATEGIES YOU CAN USE TOMORROW
(OR MAYBE EVEN TODAY, IF YOU ARE SUPER EAGER)

We, as educators, can boost divergent thinking for our students by integrating it into our daily practice. The following are specific strategies you can use as you inspire your students to think divergently.

#1: USE DIVERGENT THINKING TO GET UNSTUCK

This is a simple idea but it's one of my favorites. Pixar's Rule #9 in their *Rules of Storytelling* states, "#9: When you're stuck, make a list of what WOULDN'T happen next. Lots of times the material to get you unstuck will show up."[32] By generating a list of "bad ideas," you end up thinking divergently. You come up with random ideas that get you past your initial mental block, which can often lead to innovation. Going back to my *American Gladiators* story, my brother and I took an inventory of every single item we had that might be used to knock someone down. Our initial bad idea was the baseball bat (way too dangerous) but then we thought about adding pillows and this shifted into fluffy slippers. Quick disclaimer: don't try that at home. The baseball bat could have been far more dangerous if the duct tape failed. Regardless, divergent thinking was exactly what we needed in order to get unstuck.

You probably notice times in the classroom when students seem to hit a creative block. They might seem disengaged or even off-task but when you look a little closer, they are scared. Scared of doing things the wrong way. Scared that people won't like their work. Or maybe it's less about fear and more of a general uncertainty and a sense that they can't solve a problem. When you ask them to list "bad ideas," you reduce the fear and help them to turn off the over-analytical mind and just get their ideas out.

#2: USE DIVERGENT THINKING ACTIVITIES AS WARM-UPS AND BRAIN BREAKS

You can use divergent thinking activities as quick warm-ups to activate creativity or as a brain-break in the middle of a more analytical task. These activities can take as little as five minutes and they don't require much additional prep work.

Pareidolia: Remember when you were a kid and you would look at puffy clouds and then say something like, "That looks like a half-dragon, half-elephant eating a grilled cheese sandwich?" That was essentially a visual divergent thinking activity. It's the same thing that happens when you find the man on the moon (or the rabbit).

A classroom variation on this activity might be to show students a semi-abstract drawing and ask them to generate a list of possible ideas for what that picture might represent. Another variation on this visual divergent thinking activity is to find three different visuals and ask students to find the connections between the random objects.

Multiple Uses for Objects: Present students with two or three items and then ask them to generate a list of possible things they could make with those items. This works best when the items seem completely unrelated to one another.

Divergent Problem-Solving: Teachers can facilitate this type of divergent thinking by providing a kinesthetic problem that requires divergent thinking. A famous example is the candle challenge, where participants must stick the candle to the wall without letting any wax drip onto the ground, given only a box of tacks, a candle, and a book of matches. The answer involves placing the candle in the box of matches and using the tack to get the box onto the wall. The fascinating thing about this particular challenge is that participants nearly always solved it when the tacks were placed next to the box rather than in the box. Similarly, more participants solved the problem when the facilitator used the term "box and tacks" rather than "box of tacks." This is a powerful reminder that divergent thinking is tied to language and perspective, even when it seems to be visual and kinesthetic.

Language Play: One of my favorite language-oriented challenges is to ask students to change one letter in a sports team to make something new (so you end up with the Pittsburgh Pilates, the Dallas Cowbots or the L.A. Fakers). Here, they are working within a tight constraint to create something entirely new. Another language-oriented divergent thinking activity is to choose random items and ask students to come up with an entirely new name for them. So, again, this divergent thinking might be more visual, spatial, or language-based. However, you can easily integrate these small divergent thinking tasks into brain breaks, warm-ups, and closure activities.

#3: INTEGRATE CREATIVE CONSTRAINT INTO YOUR PROJECTS

Think outside the box. It's a popular idea. It's the story of the lone artist going away and making something radically different. But what if that's not always the case? What if creativity isn't always about thinking outside the box? What it involves thinking differently about the box? What if the most creative option is to repurpose the box? Ever watched a child play with a refrigerator box? It becomes a car, an airplane, a robot suit, a table, and a tunnel. Think of Minecraft or Legos. They are basically variations on stacking boxes. And yet, the simplicity and lack of options actually unleash the power of creativity.

This is the idea of creative constraint. It's the notion that innovation happens when you run into barriers that force you to find a new route; that creativity often involves problem-solving and systems-hacking.

Yes, creativity can mean an empty canvas or a blank page. But it can also be a roll of duct tape. It's what makes Camden Yards inherently unique. They had to incorporate the warehouse into the design. Similarly, chefs have developed some of the most creative recipes when forced to use specific ingredients. Or think of the Apollo 13 engineers who helped the astronauts back to Earth with limited time and resources. It's what makes 3 Chord Punk and live theater are so fun to experience.

When students think differently about the box, they are developing divergent thinking skills. When they have fewer resources, they have to find new ways to use the pre-existing resources. I've experienced this as a teacher and as a dad. On one occasion, we went to the beach without any lawn chairs or toys. We were so sure my kids would get bored and ask to leave. But that's not what happened. Our kids started inventing their own games. When they got tired, they created their own "sand chairs" with cup holders. Suddenly, the environment (a sandy beach) shifted from a location to a design element.

Some nuance here. "Embracing the box" doesn't mean we ignore injustice or assume that we can simply create our way out of true constraints. As educators, we need to fight against unfair practices and recognize that many students have been marginalized. We need to advocate for breaking down barriers preventing students from authentic learning. For example, we need to examine why students of color are being discipline more frequently and being recommended for gifted classes less often.

But the core idea here is that there are boxes in life – smaller constraints that present challenges. When we think divergently, we repurpose the box and innovate.

As educators, we can incorporate creative constraint in a few different ways.

Create a time constraint: In a STEM class, this might involve a quick, timed maker challenge, where they have to move through iterations quickly. In a language arts class, this might be a timed free write, where students get their words out without doing any planning in advance. The idea here is to move students quickly through the process rather that focusing on careful, deliberate planning. When this happens, students develop creative fluency, where they are able to plan, implement, and revise a creative work quickly and with a sense of agency and control.

LIFE WILL HAND YOU BOXES.
BUT OFTEN A BOX IS
AN INVITATION FOR INNOVATION.
IT'S ALL ABOUT HOW YOU THINK ABOUT IT.

Limit the materials: In chapter two, I shared the story of the two-day design faire, where students completed the Create a Sport and Create a Pinball machine challenges. The teachers provided each group with one box of random supplies. They were not allowed to use any other materials. A few students grumbled about the lack of options. However, within minutes, they were exploring how to hack the materials in unusual ways.

Limit the options: This sounds counterintuitive but sometimes the best way to spark creativity is to limit the options. I remember when I did whiteboard videos with students. They had to use the whiteboard and they had to sketch out their ideas. Their end product had to be within 30 seconds. Instead of limiting creativity, these constraints actually pushed students to think divergently.

Requiring random items: Sometimes, you might even take constraints to the next level by requiring students to use certain items (rather than merely limiting the items). If you've ever seen the TV show *Chopped,* you probably noticed that the contestants must develop their own recipes by using items that they might not typically choose. These random ingredients push the contestants to design dishes that are . . . well . . . different. Sometimes they look good different. Other times they look bizarre. But one thing is always true. These chefs are thinking divergently. I used to have students do engineering challenges with a rule that they must incorporate a specific item into their design. In creative writing, I would say something like, "your story must include robots, unicorns, and ninjas" or even "your story ends in a stinky trash compactor in the backroom of a grocery store."

#4: TRY A DIVERGENT THINKING MINI-PROJECT

When I was a kid, somebody realized that haircuts were messy, so they decided to combine a hair trimmer and vacuum cleaner. The end result was the Flow-Bee. I remember begging my mom for a Flow-Bee and she said, "no, you'll use it on the dog." And she was right. But still, the Flow-Bee is a small example of a product that uses items in an unusual way.

I mention this because sometimes students will create Flow-Bee like products. They'll make things that seem odd and quirky and you're not even sure they'll work. But that doesn't matter because, as goofy as their products might seem, there something powerful happening inside of them. They are becoming divergent thinkers.

We can help students develop this type of divergent thinking through a divergent thinking mini-project can last anywhere between 45 minutes to two hours. Students walk in to the classroom and there is a box with specific items. Individually, they think through what they might make with it.

Here's a sample prompt that helps students clarify how their project will work:

"So, here's the deal . . .

You get a stack of paper clips, some rubber bands, a marble, two sheets of paper, and three straws. Brainstorm all the things you can make with these items. Your brainstorm can be a list or a web. Go wild with this. There are no dumb ideas.

Now analyze your ideas. Combine any that seem similar. Scratch out any that you want to abandon. Mash-up any unrelated ideas that might work well together. Finally, choose one main idea from the list and make a product with it. How will your product work? What problem might it solve? How will you make it? Who is the ideal audience? Now, make this a reality! Don't forget to experiment and make tons of glorious mistakes. Each iteration takes you closer and closer to success."

Students then take their brainstorm of individual ideas and meet together in a small group to share all of their ideas. In the process, members might choose to add additional ideas as well. They might do a web, write their ideas in sticky notes, or jot them down in a shared Google Document.

Eventually, students begin to combine ideas, clarify ideas, and eventually choose one idea from the list. From there, they work through rapid prototyping to create a finished product. In the end, they can share their product in a gallery walk or present them online through a video or blog post.

Sometimes students invent something quirky and weird that they never share with an audience. In these moments, it might seem like their creative work isn't changing the world. But it is changing their world. It might not be the most original idea ever but it's original to them.

#5: CELEBRATE CREATIVE RISK-TAKING.

Divergent thinking teachers are natural creative risk-takers. Like Javi, they are willing to ask, "Why not?" instead of just asking, "Why?" And like Phyllis, they can treat each lesson as an experiment. They look at the box and say, "Why not repurpose this?"

This is what we want for our students. We want them to experiment and find new approaches to solve problems. As educators, we can develop a culture that embraces creative risk-taking. I used to work with a teacher who would ask students to share their "epic fails" with their classmates.

Students would say, "I took a creative risk by _____. It didn't work but I learned _____." Then the class would cheer afterward. His students were unafraid and, as a result, they were more likely to think divergently.

However, this also requires changes in how we assess. We can't say, "I want you to think divergently," but then use a high-stakes approach to assessment and grading. This approach to assessment will nearly always make students risk-averse. Instead, we can take a mastery-based approach where students know they'll have the chance to resubmit their work for a higher grade. When they know that they can revise their work and ultimately create something that is worth putting in a portfolio they see mistakes and revision as a natural part of the creative process. You might even add a survey or self-reflection that asks students to examine whether or not they took creative risks in their projects.

We can also celebrate creative risk-taking by embedding it inside of our projects. This was a key lesson I learned with a student named Roberto.

BE FEARLESS
IN YOUR CREATIVE WORK

FACING YOUR FEARS

Roberto showed up to my class wearing a "don't mess with me" scowl. He had already failed the eighth grade once and spent the first the previous three months at a juvenile detention center. For what it's worth, he wasn't disruptive. He never shouted across the room or talked over me when I was explaining a concept. If anything, he was completely unresponsive. I would later learn that he was facing a level of trauma that no adult, much less child, should have to face.

When Roberto refused to turn in any work during the first week, I pull him aside and asked what was going on. Nothing. Not even a shoulder shrug. The next day, I offered encouragement but this was met with pin drop silence. After two weeks without any work, I warned him that he might fail the eighth grade again. Finally, I got the shoulder shrug.

A few days later, I placed him in a group for our roller coaster challenge. Here, they had to design a model roller coaster using random supplies and a marble to simulate the car. Roberto sat on top of the desk with his arms folded and looked away. His group struggled with the project. Although they were high achievers, they spend most of the class period asking me, "Am I doing this right?" or

"Can you just give us a hint?" or even "Can we do a packet or something instead?"

Nothing seemed to work.

For the next two days, the group remained at a standstill, occasionally looking at other groups and attempting to emulate them. But then something happened. Slowly, I notice a slight change in Roberto. He uncrossed his arms and stared at the roller coaster instead of the window. A few times, he leaned in, as if he was about to say something, but then stopped mid-sentence.

Another day passed. More unreturned work. More scowls. More crossed arms.

But then something happened. On the final day of the project, he leaned forward and said, "What if . . ."

A girl gasped.

Roberto stopped midsentence and put his hand around his mouth.

"What if what?" she asked.

He shook his head.

"What if, um, I mean, this might be a stupid idea."

"It's fine," she said. "All of our ideas have been stupid. Join the club."

"What if we dropped it from a higher place, you know, and make it faster?"

"That could work," she muttered. He walked over to roller coaster and adjusted the plastic tracks.

"Actually, I have an idea, too," he continued. "What if we, uh, what if we put a gap right here and the marble kept moving? You know, it could be like the circle force we learned about."

"Like centrifugal force?" a team member asked.

"Yeah, whatever," he answered dismissively.

That afternoon, Roberto called his mom and told her he'd be staying after school. He met with his two teammates and they revised their roller coaster until the early evening, when I needed to get back home to my family.

The next morning, he met me at the door with a sketch of a revised design. "Can you give us a couple of extra days?"

I nodded.

For months, I had assumed Roberto was lazy, but he wasn't. He was afraid. The scowl masked the sheer terror he felt about all things academic. However, when he engaged in divergent thinking, he became fearless. Likewise, when he became fearless, he became a better divergent thinker.

Slowly, Roberto began turning in assignments and checking out books. He became a different student. Don't get me wrong. School remained a challenge for him for the rest of the year. In fact, he struggled through high school. However, he graduated, got into a good trade school[33], and is doing the kind work he loves to do, where he often solves hands-on problems with divergent thinking.

Ultimately, divergent thinking is all about creative risk-taking. It's about experimenting and iterating. It's about stepping away from the crowd and saying, "I have an idea. I'm not sure if it will work but I'm going to try it." But this requires courage. As the leader of your classroom, you can develop this courage in your students by creating a culture of creative risk-taking.

TRY THIS:
DIVERGENT THINKING CHALLENGE

Vintage Innovation Resources

If you're curious about divergent thinking, try a forty-minute divergent thinking challenge, where students use random objects to design something new. You can download a sample challenge in the free Vintage Innovation Toolkit at vintageinnovationbook.com/toolkit.

CHAPTER 5

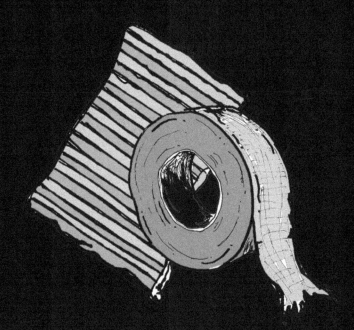

IN AN AUTOMATED WORLD, OUR STUDENTS NEED TO USE ANALOG TOOLS

When you think of innovative space travel, you might imagine the need for digital prototyping software, coding, and intricate chemistry formulas. If you want to get really geeky, you might imagine improvements in pulse plasma propulsion. And you'd be right. All of these things are necessary. But it turns out some of the most innovative designers are turning toward something a little older: origami. That's right, origami. The ancient art of paper-folding.

Researchers at NASA's Jet Propulsion Lab are constantly looking for ways to fit their spacecraft into the smallest volume possible to reduce the risk of meteorite strikes. If you have a huge spacecraft floating around, you run a higher risk of key components being punctured by giant space rocks (not the scientific term). By studying origami, engineers can design spacecraft that begins as densely packed projectiles but unfolds into a massive spacecraft. In other words, it needs to go from small and dense to massive.

Enter origami.[34]

Now, these designs are far more complicated than the paper cranes and Cootie Catchers you grew up folding in the fourth grade when you played MASH. However, at its core, this is still origami. Manan Arya[35], dubbed the "oragamist in chief" by his peers at NASA, studies origami using complex computer programs but ultimately, it all comes down to the folding. He takes a vintage innovation approach combining computer modeling and modern mathematics research with an ancient artform and analog materials.

A fellow designer, Robert Salazar puts it this way, "With most origami, the magic comes from the folding."[36] Salazar's obsession with origami began as a child, after reading the children's book A Thousand Paper Cranes[37]. His story is a bold reminder of the power way fiction can inspire future generations of innovators. But Salazar's story is also a reminder of the power of hands-on learning that actually involves your own two hands.

WE NEED OLD SCHOOL TOOLS

We live in an era of automation. Factories that once housed thousands of workers are now buzzing with rows of robots[38]. With machine learning and artificial intelligence, the robots are learning to communicate, iterate, and improve in their performance.[39] Many school leaders are responding to this reality by purchasing high-tech fabrication equipment and investing in state-of-the-art makerspaces.[40] However, in the rush to be high-tech, there's a danger in the Astrodome Effect, where we embrace gadgetry and futurism only to find that the tools grow obsolete within a decade. While there's certainly a benefit from using the newest available technology, there's also a high risk in abandoning all things analog.

I learned this lesson the hard way in my third year of teaching. Back in 2005, I decided to "go paperless" with my middle school social studies class. I spent the summer designing curriculum that would incorporate blogging, podcasts, shared documents (back when Google Docs was still Writely), and other cloud-based tools. No pen. No paper. No books. Just computers zipping along on Linux.

AT SOME POINT,
HANDS-ON LEARNING SHOULD
INCLUDE USING YOUR ACTUAL

HANDS

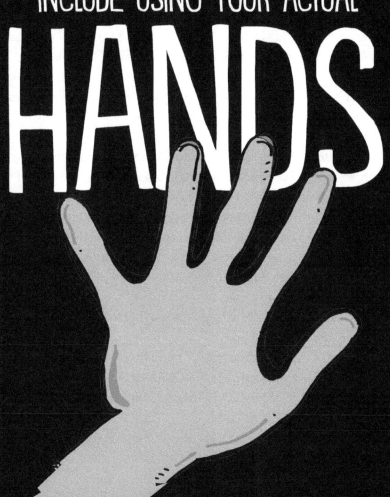

The schoolyear launched with a rush of excitement. Students would show up before and after school. They rushed through the hallways to get to class early. This was the future. I had nailed it. But then something happened. I noticed that my students weren't talking to each other as much before school. Instead, they were playing web-based games. Rather than creating content, they watched videos. As the weeks wore on, the novelty wore off. Students no longer showed up early, eager to use the new devices.

Finally, a student pulled me aside and said, "I miss last year."

"What?" I asked defensively.

"I miss the debates we used to have. I miss the Socratic Seminars. Remember those?"

I nodded.

"Plus, some of this is boring. It took me three days to do a concept map on the computer. Last year, we used yarn to connect the ideas. Remember that?" He was right. We had used different colored strings of yard to connect concepts from World War I by wrapping them around meter sticks and discussing the connections between ideas. It was frenetic, tactile, and collaborative.

"But you can go back and look at the concept map you made," I pointed out.

"I guess so. But will I actually do that? I feel like I remembered it better when we used yarn."

"I hadn't thought about that," I admitted.

"We had a paper fight for the Civil War. Remember that?"

Remember it? How could I forget? I had spent my entire prep period picking up paper balls.

He continued, "You let us sketch out our notes instead of having to type them. Could we swap with another classroom? Just for a day or two?"

"You want to ditch the computers?" I asked.

"I mean, not forever. Just for a few days."

This student was right. In my rush to create a paperless class-room, I had designed the Astrodome. So I decided to bring back the vintage tools and resources we had used before. We didn't abandon the computers. We continued to do podcasts, documen-taries, and blogs. But we also used whiteboards and paper journals with sketchnotes. We swapped classrooms with other teachers, so we could do physical simulations and games and they could use computers. We had regular discussions, debates, and Socratic Seminars. We also did analog and high-tech mashups like white-board videos and Socratic-style podcasts. I had made the mistake of being tech-driven rather than learner-driven.

TECH-DRIVEN   LEARNER-DRIVEN

I learned the hard way that relevance isn't about using the lat-est available technology. It's about solving the latest problems by leveraging whatever technology works best. It's counterintuitive but sometimes an older tool or strategy might actually be the most relevant because it's so different. Sometimes you need to fold some origami to design the most state-of-the-art spacecraft.

FIVE REASONS TO EMBRACE VINTAGE TOOLS

A few months ago, I visited an amazing makerspace at Germantown Academy in Pennsylvania. Students could move seamlessly through the space craft maker projects. They used the LAUNCH cycle to do larger design thinking projects. The students had access to computers, tablets, and 3D printers. They worked collaboratively on robotics projects. However, they strategically chose analog tools as well. Students hammered things together. They used duct tape to prototype. They had yarn and paper and markers. It was a true vintage innovation mash-up.

I asked Jessica Killo, the designer of the space, why she used lo-fi tools and she answered, "Sometimes those tools are more developmentally appropriate. We need to design the space to meet students where they are at developmentally. But also, sometimes vintage tools can do a better job inspiring creative thinking."

#1
VINTAGE TOOLS CAN ENCOURAGE DIVERGENT THINKING AND CREATIVITY

Camden Yards worked because the engineers and architects incorporated the limitations into the design. Similarly, when students use low-tech tools, they have to work within the creative constraints of the available tools. In the process, they engage in divergent thinking because they no longer have unlimited options.

When I taught journalism, we had a green screen that allowed students to have any background they wanted. Students could also use Final Cut to create highly produced videos that would look professional. However, their best videos were often the sketch-note videos they created with pens, paper, and cell phones. I watched students use folds, tears, and sketched-out symbols in original ways as they conveyed big ideas in their short videos. These videos were more creative because students had to incorporate the creative constraint into their design. Note that these were not tech-free projects. Students still used computers for research. They often wrote their scripts on a shared document. They filmed their videos with their smartphones. However, they embraced the vintage element of drawing by hand.

Similarly, in STEM, the "tinkering" approach often blends low-tech tools (like cardboard) with high-tech tools like circuitry or programming.[41]

#2
WHEN STUDENTS ARE MAKING THINGS BY HAND, THEY ARE A PART OF THE ENTIRE PROCESS.

Sometimes the technology does too much of the heavy lifting for students. At times, a 3D printer can work almost like Guitar Hero. You think you are making something physical but you're really just pushing the buttons. I've seen STEM classes where students take free templates from the internet and printing them off without making many modifications. While the end result looked impressive, the students haven't actually engaged in creative thinking.

By contrast, when students prototype by hand, they have a better sense of the actual physics involved in prototyping. They can use a digital model to create a roller coaster and test it out using a simulation. However, when they make tiny tweaks to the roller coaster that they're building by hand, they get to feel it evolve and experience it in a more temporal way. This doesn't mean we abandon 3D printers. But it is a reminder that we shouldn't abandon duct tape and cardboard for 3D printers and filament.

In some of my favorite makerspaces, students prototype with analog, lo-fi tools first before they move into the more abstract realm of digital modeling and 3D printers. In other words, if you're doing a STEAM / STEM challenge, you might have students prototype first with their lo-fi tools, allowing them to think through ideas and see and feel the iterations evolving. Then, when it's done, they can move into digital modeling and 3D printing.

#3
SOMETIMES LOW-TECH IS MORE DEVELOPMENTALLY APPROPRIATE.

Younger students especially need to make things with their bare hands. It won't be as polished, but they will learn in a way that fits human development. There's a very real danger in asking students to use abstract programs when they are still in a more concrete phase developmentally.[42] We might want to have students using manipulatives in math rather than using math apps on their tablets. We can still have young students type a blog post or make a video, but we also want journals and small group discussions.

#4
OFTEN ANALOG TOOLS ARE FASTER AND CHEAPER.

For all the talk of students being digital natives, advanced programs are often complex to learn, which can be a challenge for teachers with limited time (which is pretty much every teacher ever). For visual design, it can take months to learn the ins and outs of Photoshop. In engineering, the 3D modeling programs often require multiple direct instruction lessons and a series of tutorials. Even something as simple as a concept mapping program can take three to four times as long to create compared to the paper-based version. It requires additional cognitive load for students to learn a new software application and when this happens, it not only takes longer, but it also reduces students' ability to focus on the learning task at hand.

But also, the analog tools are often cheaper, which means there's less of a pressure to use them on a regular basis. When schools purchase expensive technology, teachers often feel obligated to make sure they're "getting their money's worth," which can lead to a tech-driven rather than a student-driven focus. But with vintage tools, the lower costs mean teachers feel the freedom to use a broader variety of resources and abandon a tool that isn't working.

#5
WHEN STUDENTS USE ANALOG TOOLS, THE LEARNING STICKS

Each time I get a new cohort, I have students who scoff at my suggestion that they take notes with their laptops closed. After all, I'm the techie professor. However, handwritten notes force you to slow down and actually provide more options. You can change sizes and styles, sketch out visuals, and make diagrams more smoothly by hand than with typed notes. According to the research, handwritten notes can improve conceptual development and lead to a higher retention of information compared to typed notes.[43] Similarly, elementary students improve in their mathematical thinking when using hands-on manipulatives. [44]

This doesn't mean we need to toss out our video studios and makerspaces and replace them with boxes of duct tape and cardboard. After all, with a vintage innovation approach, you still use newer technology, but it's coupled with older, analog tools in a way that prioritizes the learning. Instead of asking, "how can the technology transform the learning?" you're asking, "How can this learning transform how we use our technology?"

So, you write sketchnotes but you also blog in your third-grade class. You have Socratic Seminars but you also record podcasts in that middle school social studies class. You blend together physical prototyping and 3D modeling in your high school engineering course.

What does this look like?

There are tons of opportunities to use vintage tools in your classroom.

Consider Lam Nyguyen. He teaches some of the most complex, advanced mathematics courses I've ever seen. These are the kinds of courses that can sometimes come across as daunting and impossible. But his students are confident as they master the content. When I visited his classroom, I was surprised to see such an abstract subject being taught in such a hands-on way.

I asked him about his philosophy of technology. "The first thing is I only use tech when it helps us do things that are otherwise impossible."

"What do you mean by this?" I asked.

"We use spreadsheets and it makes things move more quickly. We use 3-D models to animate concepts and visualize formulas. We obviously use calculators. But the goal is to use these only when it truly works better than a low-tech version."

"So, when is it better to use something physical?"

"At a younger age, they need physical models. They need manipulatives. But even in my high school classes, I want students to hold it, pick it up, play with it. Math isn't something in your head.

It's something in our world. It's something you should hold in your hands."

"But you obviously use a lot of technology in your classroom as well," I pointed out.

"You should use the tech until you push it to your max. Go with the lowest abstraction possible. You should max out the low fi until you see its limitations and then you go to tech."

When I watched his students, I noticed how often they moved from hands-on models to digital models seamlessly. They sketched ideas out on whiteboards and then moved to a complex computer program. It reminded me of the origami rocket scientists at NASA. His students were embracing a vintage innovation approach to math.

THE POWER OF PHYSICAL PROTOTYPING

Melissa Deutsch is a master PBL teacher. As a classroom teacher, instructional coach, and professor, she has done groundbreaking work on how to design projects where every student can actively participate. The other day, she shared a story of a fourth-grade student who took a creative risk.

"I'll never forget Cassie's final project. Cassie wasn't exactly a "high-achiever" in the traditional sense, and her work ethic wasn't exemplary. But she did enjoy the book she chose. She had been reading 'Dear Mr. Henshaw,' a story about a young boy in sixth grade named Leigh Botts."

Melissa empowered her students to design projects that would reflect the story they had read. As she described it, "When Cassie had the opportunity to choose anything for her final project, she completely went above and beyond any 'menu of choices' I could have provided. She made a plan, sketched it out, and had a conference with me to see if we could get the materials she needed. And then she went to work. She created a model of the semi-truck out of paper and a cereal box she had brought from home. She painted the cab, the trailer, and even the tires with paints and brushes I found in a storage closet. She made the tires move with brad fasteners (every teacher has a million of those in their desk)."

In other words, Cassie used lo-fi, everyday tools to prototype something powerful. She even wrote a diary from the perspective of the truck describing Leigh's experience with divorce, loneliness, and isolation.

"The truck would cry at sad songs on long drives. How excited the dad would get on weekends he got to pick up Leigh. And how upset he would get when something along the drive would cause a back-up and he wouldn't be able to follow through on his promises to his son."

Melissa's project begins with this idea of creative constraint. She was in an environment where they didn't have the best technology or the greatest resources. However, she empowered a student to work within the constraints to design a meaningful project. The lo-fi tools were part of the solution, not the problems.

THE POWER OF THE MASH-UP

While Melissa's classroom emphasized the analog tools, often the solution is a mash-up between vintage and modern.

VINTAGE	MODERN	MASH-UP
Sketches	Video	Sketch Videos
Journals	Blogs	Visual Blogging
Socratic Seminar	Podcast	Debate Podcasts
Cardboard proto-typing	3D printer	Blended divergent thinking challenge
Guest speakers	Video recording	Video history projects
Lo-fi materials	Circuitry	Tinkering projects

Note that this isn't ground-breaking. You often see these forms of vintage innovation in schools all around the world. But these projects are ground-breaking to students and the fact that you see them often in schools doesn't negate the profound ways these activities impact students in their creative development.

YOU DON'T NEED A 3D PRINTER TO HAVE A GREAT MAKERSPACE

YES, 3D PRINTERS ARE GREAT BUT SO ARE ANALOG TOOLS

CREATING A VINTAGE INNOVATION MAKERSPACE

Often when I lead a design thinking workshop, a participant will ask, "What if I don't have a fancy maker space?" Another variation is, "I don't have a 3D printer. Can I still have a makerspace?" Yes, and yes. It's not about the technology. Yes, technology is great. With our smart phones, we can do things that were once unimaginable. But the real power is in the creative process. Sometimes the high-tech gadgetry can actually get in the way of creative thinking while the simplicity and physicality of the analog tools can inspire innovation.

I recently visited a high-tech multimillion dollar university makerspace. At first, I noticed the CAD machines whirring and the 3D printers printing and I secretly worried that I had failed my former STEAM students by failing to teach them how to use this technology. A few engineering students pointed to a touchscreen and argued about the ideal method for digital modeling. But then something caught my eye.

Duct tape (aka the greatest technology ever invented). Okay, it didn't *literally* catch my eye. That would have been painful. But I noticed students attempting to solve a complex problem using duct tape and cardboard. At another table, students sifted through a box of washers and gears and grommets.

Meanwhile, another student pulled out a sketchbooks and a sharpened pencil and began sketching out a prototype. A team of students huddled around a blank white wall covered in neon sticky notes as they debated potential design solutions. Others scribbled frantically on whiteboards.

This moment reminded me that a makerspace isn't about high-tech gadgetry. It's about problem-solving and collaboration. A makerspace is simply a location where students are engaging in creative thinking and hands-on making. The theater is a makerspace. The auto shop is a makerspace. The library is a makerspace. The art room is a makerspace. While these spaces vary immensely, there is a common theme. People are using vintage and modern tools to create something new.

TRY THIS:
SKETCH-NOTE VIDEOS

Sketch-note videos are a powerful mash-up of old-school and new-school. Students can share explanatory videos showing how to engage in a process or how a particular concept works. You can use these in any subject and any grade level. To get started on sketch-note videos, check out the Vintage Innovation Toolkit at vintageinnovationbook.com/toolkit.

CHAPTER 6

IN A WORLD OF ARTIFICIAL INTELLIGENCE, OUR STUDENTS NEED PHILOSOPHY

Imagine you are building a self-driving car. Chances are you'll look for a team of top-notch engineers who can solve complex problems. You'll probably recruit software engineers and mechanical engineers and experts in user interface (UI) and user experience (UX) design.

But then you realize that people won't drive this car in a lab. Context matters. Suddenly, you're dealing with messy cultural, social, and political issues that you can't anticipate in a controlled lab setting. Take a dark example. This self-driving is cruising down the road. A man runs in front of it. If you swerve, you'll cause a potentially deadly accident. If you don't, the results could be equally disastrous[45]. In this moment, you need something that artificial intelligence can't generate.

Wisdom.

For years, technology companies operated with a socially neutral mindset. Take a problem and engineer your way to a solution. Focus on the *how* and leave the *why* to the public.

But things are starting to change. As our technology continues to grow more complicated, corporations are beginning to embrace the human element. It's one thing for Google to say, "Don't be evil." It's another thing for Google to ask the very hard question, "What is evil?"

Suddenly, the most cutting-edge technology companies are turning toward something timeless to solve their most pressing problems. They are reaching out to the humanities to deal with these deeply human issues.[46] [47] [48] As technology companies shift toward embracing the humanities, they are beginning to seek out job candidates with a background in philosophy to answer the kinds of questions that can't be solved with high-tech engineering.

It's as if tech companies, pushing toward the future at breakneck speeds are now facing whiplash and turning back to something deeply vintage. Suddenly, the Silicon Valley CEOs are seeking out philosophers to answer questions they were too busy to ask as our society hurled toward the future. [49] [50] They're geeking out on Seneca and stoicism,[51] which Tim Ferris describes it as, "an ideal operating system for thriving in high-stress environments."[52]

WHY PHILOSOPHY IS ACTUALLY THE SUBJECT OF THE FUTURE

When you think of the "subject of the future," you might imagine coding or engineering or maybe something to do with artificial intelligence. However, while those subjects can help us solve the "how?" questions, students will need philosophy to answer the "why?" questions.

This is why philosophy is so critical. It is a vintage discipline that ties together all subjects and all disciplines. The following are key reasons philosophy is actually the subject of the future.

BIG IDEA #1
PHILOSOPHY IS VITAL IN AN AGE OF ARTIFICIAL INTELLIGENCE.

Artificial intelligence continues to blur the lines between ourselves and our machines. What does it mean to have an original thought? What does this mean for plagiarism and copyright? How do you make sense out of ideas like attribution and originality?

We are still in the early years of AI. Currently, companies are developing AI to write news articles.[53] We'll see an increase in AI products around budgeting and other analytical jobs. Here's where wisdom becomes critical. Students need to be prepared to think in ways that transcend artificial intelligence. As we shift toward more augmented reality and virtual reality, our students will need to ask about the nature of reality. Further, as technological innovations make it easy to craft misinformation and "deep fake" videos grow more prevalent, our students will need the logic and critical thinking of philosophy to view information wisely.

BIG IDEA #2
PHILOSOPHY HELPS US OUT OF ECHO CHAMBERS

Social media relevance filters[54] are creating echo chambers that shape how we view truth. Most of our students begin consuming content at a young age. Platforms like YouTube will move to related videos and playlists automatically. As they move toward Facebook and Twitter, the algorithms determine the new content shown; not by accuracy of information but by relatedness and relevance. As a result, children grow up with a worldview shaped in part by an algorithm that narrows down their filter. This creates an echo chamber that limits divergent viewpoints.

Echo chambers can exist in communities as well – whether it's a family or a neighborhood or a religious institution. But the beauty of a classroom is that you have a group of students from various backgrounds and a variety of worldviews. When you ask students to think like philosophers, you widen their worldview and you guide them out of their echo chambers. In this sense, a classroom is one of the last truly diverse locations for ideas.

BIG IDEA #3
PHILOSOPHY IS TIMELESS IN AN AGE OF INSTANT INFORMATION.

We live in a world of amusement and novelty. Trends shift quickly. Information spreads rapidly. But there are some things that remain timeless. People will always fall in love. They will have weddings and funerals and birthday parties. They will stub their toes and curse into the heavens. They will get angry when they're hungry and they will cuddle close to those they love. They'll get lonely and lost when they feel misunderstood.

Critics are quick to say that technology has made us shallow and narcissist.[55] They point to the Instagram feeds with selfies and pictures of food as evidence that our technology is ruining our world. But recently I visited a museum and guess what I saw? Lots of pictures of food. Tons of them. And even more selfies. True, they were called "self-portraits," but they were selfies.

This visit to the museum reminded me that we, as humans, aren't all that different from those in the past. True, our world is changing. But our basic human needs remain the same. And that's why we need philosophy. It is timeless because it cuts to the core of our most fundamental philosophical questions. These are the questions that we asked a thousand years ago and we still ask now: What is reality? What is truth? What does it mean to be human? What is the purpose of life?

There is a chorus of voices from the past and, if we're open to it, these thinkers raise some great questions for us to grapple with. And I guess that's the point. It's not that we buy into one specific philosophy but that we learn how to engage in philosophical dialogue. The cool thing about Socrates is not that he finds the answers. In fact, he almost never does. Rather, it's that he asks all the right questions. Within a culture of instant information, where our smartphones can give us fast answers, philosophy reminds us that some answers can't be answered quickly.

As educators, we shouldn't limit our sources to famous philosophers. Our students can explore the writings, speeches, and the art of activists from marginalized groups who raised hard philosophical questions in order to spark change in the world.

SIRI AND ALEXA CAN HELP YOU
ANSWER QUESTIONS,

BUT PHILOSOPHY WILL HELP YOU
QUESTION ANSWERS

THE WAY WE THINK ABOUT THINKING

Your mind is not a computer. That's pretty obvious, right? However, when we talk about the brain, we tend to borrow language from the latest available technology. I'll get to that in a moment, but first, let me nerd out on linguistics for just a moment. I promise it will relate to the classroom . . . eventually.

We are immersed in world of unspoken metaphors. These metaphors shape the language we use as we make sense out of reality. This is a key idea of the Conceptual Metaphor Theory. According to this theory, conceptual metaphors shape the way we perceive reality, communicate with one another, think about ideas, and, ultimately, act.[56] The words cluster together into a semantic web, leading some cognitive linguists to hypothesize that that the conceptual domain corresponds to the neural mapping of the brain.[57]

These metaphors tend to go unnoticed. However, they are powerful. For example, you can easily detect when a conversation is becoming an argument by the use of war metaphors. People use phrases like, "Don't get defensive" or mention "being offensive." They use the term "heated" and might mention "choosing battles." Often, you are asked to "take sides" and you might find yourself "shooting down" another person's ideas.

You see the Conceptual Metaphor Theory at work in the way folks talk about education. Some view it as a science and use terms like "theory" and "assessment instruments" while others view teaching as an artform or a craft.

Humans have historically described the mind (and often the brain) using the latest available technology. In ancient China, Confucius described the mind as a container. To Confucius, the mind was capable of both hiding and holding objects.[58]

The Greeks used hydraulic pumps to describe mental processes and wax tablets to describe memory. The ancient Hebrew writer Jeremiah used the metaphor or a diamond stylus on a stone tablet. With the dawn of the printing press, John Locke used the term tabula rasa, or empty page, to describe the mind. While the differences are subtle, printing on a white paper conveys more permanence and shifts toward a more standardized, mechanical view of the mind. Later, philosophers used mechanical metaphors, including clocks, to describe the mind. We still use the term "chain of thought" (first coined by Hobbes at the dawn of the Enlightenment) and describe being "derailed" or "off track."

When we use a phrase like, "I see what you mean," or "I'm trying to picture it," there is the idea of thinking as an act of visualization. However, as technology has evolved, we have adopted newer ways to describe this visualization process. We now use phrases like "snapshot," "filter," and "worldview" to describe the visual element of thinking.

As we began to understand the role of neurons and mental processes, scientists adopted the language of newer emerging technologies. By the late 1800's, German physicist Hermann von Helmholtz used the telegraph metaphor to describe cognition.[59] Half a century later, when Otto Loewi used the language of the telegraph and radio to describe his discovery of the first neurotransmitter while experimenting with frogs. Thus, the brain was able to "send signals" to other neurons.[60]

Fast forward to now (note my accidental use of a video metaphor to describe time). We refer to "information processing" and "neural networks." We use terms like "storage" and "retrieval" when describing learning. We discuss how humans are "hardwired." This might not seem significant. However, there are huge implications for the techno-futurism that fuels (again, machine metaphor) the way we talk about the brain.

Our brains are not computers. We do not process information so much as engage in sense-making. Learning is a deeply emotional and social endeavor. Computers cannot engage in divergent thinking. They cannot convey empathy. Consider the role of simple recall. A computer can always recall specific information but for our students, it often requires a trigger or some kind. This is why we use things like mnemonic devices and acronyms to help with this process.

Or consider the role of memory. Your brain does not store and retrieve memories. Instead, each time you recall a memory, you re-imagine it. While we use phrases like "picturing it," a memory is never a snapshot and each retelling is an evolution.

Here's why it's critical that we pay attention to the voices of the past. The Greek's viewed memory as a wax tablet. Socrates described the process this way, "Let us, then, say that this is the gift of Memory, the mother of the Muses, and that whenever we wish to remember anything we see or hear or think of in our own minds, we hold this wax under the perceptions and thoughts and imprint them upon it, just as we make impressions from seal rings; and whatever is imprinted we remember and know as long as its image lasts, but whatever is rubbed out or cannot be imprinted we forget and do not know."[61]

As we think about the corruption of memory in each recall, the process is much closer to a malleable wax tablet than it is a file stored in a hard drive. When we make sense out of social-emotional learning and the role of trauma, a wax tablet feels more accurate than a computer chip. In fact, there are neuroscientists right now who believe that the computer metaphor and its inherent semantic environment is holding back neuroscience and our understanding of the brain[62].

In other words, although we need to be up to date on research, we need metaphors from the past to help pull us out of the echo chambers of the present.

YOUR BRAIN IS NOT A
COMPUTER

WHAT DOES THIS MEAN FOR TEACHERS?

Philosophy isn't merely a mental exercise. It's ultimately about the values we hold, the decisions we make, and the actions we take. When we teach students how to be philosophers, we encourage them to become the strategic thinkers and the life-long learners we want them to be. They can have a framework for making sense out of a world that can sometimes feel like science fiction. But what does this actually look like?

Here are some of the ways you can integrate philosophy into the curriculum:

#1
QUESTION EVERYTHING

Encourage them to question answers as often as they answer questions. Teach students to identify the bias in a source and to pick apart the information to make sense out of worldview and philosophical underpinnings.

Start with student inquiry. Kids are inherently philosophical. They are asking "why" at a young age. Encourage these questions and watch as they grow more and more philosophical. Don't shy away from bigger questions that don't have immediate answers. Sometimes kids have a hard time with the idea that they won't have the answer at the end of a philosophical inquiry.

#2
TEACH PHILOSOPHICAL REASONING WITHIN YOUR CONTENT AREA

Philosophy is not a subject area. It's a way of thinking that exists within every subject. Here's a sample of what it might mean in your subject area:

Science: Is technology more positive or negative? Can all truth be discovered scientifically? What ethics should guide scientific discovery?

Math: What is the danger in treating math as socially neutral? How do people use numbers to manipulate others? What is the best way to solve _____ problem?

Language Arts: What does it mean to be human? What is truth and how do you discover it?

Social Studies: How is technology reshaping our world? What is the purpose of government? What is more important: freedom or safety?

Foreign Language: What is the power of language? How does language shape culture? How does the ability to communicate impact our understanding of humanity?

The Arts: How does art reflect life? How does it change life? What is the purpose of art?

Philosophy is a way of thinking that impacts how you view your world and ultimately how you live. When we integrate philosophy into our subjects, we not only help develop philosophical thinkers. We also demonstrate that the topics we teach are vital to life.

Note that while many of the previous examples fit most closely with secondary classrooms, students at a younger age can discuss the deeper questions within their subjects. Sometimes they need some additional modeling. At a younger age, your philosophy discussions are often tied to more concrete ideas. Many teachers use picture books to launch deeper philosophical discussions. At this level, it might not even "look" like philosophy in a traditional sense. But make no mistake, when students learn to think philosophically, they are better equipped to make sense out of a rapidly changing world.

I know a second-grade teacher (who has chosen to remain anonymous) from my former school district who empowers her students to think like philosophers. As a teacher of color, she wants her students to see books that not only reflected her students' lived experience but would also expand their worldview. She begins the discussions by reading a culturally-responsive picture book and asking students to make connections between the text, themselves, and their world. What begins as a book discussion evolves into conversations about bigger philosophical ideas like truth and fairness. She asks students to explain their thinking and she provides sample sentences to help them engage in the discussion and access the language.

When I asked her about it, she said, "I want them to see that stories have meaning. Yes, I'm covering standards. But we're going deeper than that. I want them to become deeper thinkers and see a bigger world." While her students might not have realized it at the time, they were becoming philosophers.

#3
USE SOCRATIC SEMINARS

Let students argue with one another. Really. As a teacher, my natural inclination is to shy away from conflict and keep the peace. However, I've learned that it's better to have students share conflicting ideas and learn to listen respectfully to divergent ideas. Class culture is critical here. It's important that they feel safe as they engage in these contentious conversations. But these are the conversations that expand one's worldview and lead to deeper wisdom.

One strategy is to set aside time for philosophical conversations. When I taught social studies, I used to do a Philosophical Friday every other week. Students would engage in structured Socratic Seminars where they sat in a circle and wrestled with the deeper questions that connected to our content. Even when our class shifted toward project-based learning and design thinking, we would take breaks from our projects and focus on philosophy.

#4
USE PHILOSOPHY TO MAKE SENSE OF TECHNOLOGY

If we want students to make sense out of a connected world, we need to integrate technology criticism questions into our daily use of technology. Digital citizenship is about more than simply being nice online. It's about making sense of the way technology is reshaping our world. Acceptable use is about more than being safe online. It's about using technology wisely. This is why it helps to ask critical thinking questions about the technology and how it's shaping our world.

STUDENTS AS PHILOSOPHERS

In an era where we can find information anywhere, students need to grow in wisdom. In an era where we are constantly redefining what is possible and what is real, students need wrestle with the hard questions around the nature of reality. At a time when worldviews are being shaped by algorithms and relevance filters, our students will need to think big and step outside of the social media echo chambers to wrestle with hard questions. In other words, we need students to be philosophers. As teachers, we can craft the experiences that make this a reality.

TRY THIS:
SOCRATIC SEMINAR

One starting place is the Socratic Seminar structure. It's an open, democratic style of philosophical discussion. It can work at any grade level with any subject. You can download it from the Vintage Innovation Toolkit at vintageinnovationbook.com/toolkit.

CHAPTER 7

IN A CONNECTED WORLD, OUR STUDENTS NEED TO DEVELOP
EMPATHY

For the last few decades, the American Girl company has designed ever more inclusive dolls. I remember hearing my former students describe what it was like to finally see a girl who was Latino, Asian, or African-American.

Still, it took someone outside of the organization to see a group of children who didn't have dolls that represented them – namely children who had prosthetic arms or legs. That's when the team at A Step Ahead Prosthetics began customizing American Girl dolls so that children could have dolls that more fully represented them.[63]

This solution was innovative, not because it required the newest, state-of-the-art technology but because it began with empathy. On a technical level, a prosthetic limb isn't that challenging to add to a doll. But on a human level, it's a powerful innovation.

Empathy isn't a new concept. For thousands of years, some of the greatest thinkers have reminded us to look outside ourselves and build empathy with others. Even our term "compassion" originally meant "to suffer together."[64] It wasn't about pity. It was about shared experiences, mutual respect, and concrete action.

Dr. Sarah Thomas makes a distinction between empathy and false compassion. She mentions, "There is no room for pity in empathy" and describes how true empathy requires viewing others as equal and showing mutual respect.[65] Thomas warns about empathy that resorts to Othering which involves "someone centering him/herself as the hero and saving the day, regardless of whether their "saving" is welcomed and solicited, or not."

Genuine empathy is vital to innovation. The quality of your creative work improves when you design with empathy in mind. In fact, the Stanford d.School begins their design thinking model with empathy.[66] Similarly, when students begin with empathy, they are able to craft products, services, and art that actually reflect the needs and desires of an authentic audience.

WHEN WE DESIGN FROM A PLACE OF EMPATHY, IT HAS THE POWER TO CHANGE THE

WORLD

But this has to involve the type of mutual respect Sarah Thomas describes. Tim Brown of IDEO describes it this way, "It's not 'us versus them' or even 'us on behalf of them.' For a design thinker, it has to be 'us with them.'"[67]

WHY EMPATHY MATTERS

For a full semester, my students engaged in design thinking projects that incorporated service learning elements. Our students had walked through what eventually became the Launch Cycle.[68] We had focused on empathy and the intersection of design thinking and service learning. After serving our local community and doing larger global projects, a student pitched an idea to us.

"What if we created something for the people who clean the classrooms? Like, what's the name of the person who cleans our room?"

Busted.

"Uh . . . I . . . I . . . I don't know," I answered after standing there in awkward silence.

"Maybe you should," she answered.

She was right. This was a wake-up call for me. For all the talk of empathy, I had failed to truly appreciate the person who served our school in such a tangible way. So, I learned our the names of our custodial crew and I began to learn the story of the woman who cleaned our room each day.

This was also the start of a service project. A group of students wrote thank you notes and put together gift baskets. They brought in items they had bought from Wal-Mart or the Dollar Store. Even though we were a Title One school in a low-income community, our students were wildly generous. One afternoon, we placed the gift baskets in the classrooms. My students waited nervously.

Minutes later, we watched as our hardworking custodial crew walked out carrying their gifts.

It was a reminder of all the people in schools who work tirelessly to care for our students. Often, the first person they meet is a crossing guard, who stands out in the freezing cold to guarantee students get there safely or a bus driver who braves the weather and the traffic and hundreds of screaming kids to get students to school on time. It has me thinking about the aides who help ensure that all students learn, the custodians who transform a well-worn school into something beautiful, and the secretaries who keep things running every day. It has me thinking about the nurses who respond not only to small cuts and bruises but to bigger medical issues as well. They build relationships and take care of the whole child. There are so many hard-working staff members who make school work. Every. Single. Day.

OUR WORLD NEEDS EMPATHY

We live in a world in dire need of empathy. Log onto social media and you'll see sharp barbs tossed back and forth. You'll see people shouting in echo chambers without taking the time to listen. You'll see trolls tearing people down for the fun of it. You'll see dark stories revealing the worst in humanity. It's easy in these moments to feel hopeless.

But there's also a hidden opportunity. As dark as the discourse may be, this is also an opportunity for kindness, for understanding, and for action. As a teacher, you can help develop empathy in your students.

There's a practical element at work here as well. When students develop empathy, learn how to collaborate with others. They become better listeners. Here, they can become better global citizens by as they interact with people from diverse backgrounds. This, in turn, exposes them to new ideas and sharpens their critical thinking. Often, they become more self-reflective and even humble as they consider how their actions impact others.

As a former middle school teacher, I've noticed that my most empathetic students had an easier time embracing diverse populations and ideas when they went to college and entered the workforce. In a connected world, they knew that had mastered greatest connection of all – the human connection.

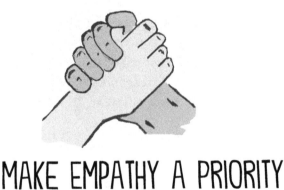

MAKE EMPATHY A PRIORITY

There's a danger in false empathy. It's the kind of empathy that occurs when people ignore injustice and when they refuse to pay attention to power dynamics. For me, it took a student with wide eyes, who paid attention to the least recognized and least powerful members in our school – the cleaning crew. This student called me out for it — and rightfully so. In the process, she exposed my arrogance and ignorance and inability to see. As educators, we need these humbling moments so that we can develop deeper empathy.

So, how do we get there? How do we develop real empathy rather than false empathy?

I was recently talking to a few friends of mine who have devoted their lives to empathy and equity. I asked them about what it means to show empathy as a teacher and how to help students develop it as well.

Model it. You can help create a culture of empathy by showing empathy toward students. Listen to them. Ask for their input in lessons. Encourage them to help create the class procedures and rules. As a middle school team leader, I ran a weekly student leadership meeting where students would volunteer to generate project ideas and essential questions. They would go over data from student surveys and help us, as a team, to come up with next steps. You can also honor their agency by letting them choose topics or questions. Use surveys frequently and talk about how those results are informing your instructional decision. But it goes deeper than that. The most empathetic teachers I know are able to apologize to students when they make mistakes. They know how to wait before rushing judgment.

Understand the role of silence. There's a fantastic Edutopia article by Jose Vilson on empathy and collaboration. He writes about the need for silence and space as a strategy for building empathy in students.[69]

Integrate it. Teachers can integrate empathy into subjects like math and science, helping students see that these subjects are human-oriented and connected to real contexts. When this happens, it becomes easier to focus on empathy in design projects as well.

Embrace the power of story. Stories can be a powerful way to help students build empathy because they help students learn to see other perspectives in a way that's safe. In a previous chapter, I shared the story of a teacher who leads philosophical discussions based on culturally-relevant picture books. Through this process, her students are developing empathy. Each book is an opportunity to bring in the human element and help students gain exposure to others' experiences.

Pay attention to power dynamics. When students are truly designing from a place of empathy, they will run into injustice. It's important that we avoid glossing over the injustice or treating it as something easily fixable. This is why empathy in education needs to overlap with cultural humility and culturally responsive teaching. Which leads to my next thought . . .

Avoid the temptation to "create for." Empathy is two-sided and horizontal. But when we slip into a "design for" mindset, we're not showing empathy. We're showing pity. When we fail to show humility, we run the risk of designing products people will not actually use or even causing new unanticipated barriers.

Admit that it's challenging. Empathy doesn't always come naturally to us. It's easy to miss the people around us or get stuck in our own perceptions. This is why it helps to have hard conversations about the challenges of showing empathy.

There are some great strategies for developing student empathy within design thinking. Students can do Needs Assessments, A Day in the Life, a sketch-note of needs, or a needs-wants chart (which you can access in the Vintage Innovation Toolkit at vintage-innovationbook.com/toolkit). However, none of these structures will work unless we create the groundwork ahead of time to help students develop empathy. It needs to be a daily part of our classroom culture. When I interviewed Dr. Thomas, she described it this way, "To have true empathy means a shift in your teaching so that you're using culturally sustainable practices." This impacts everything from discipline to the selection of materials to the way we examine our own implicit biases.

EMPATHY IN EACH SUBJECT

So, what does empathy actually look like in each subject area?

- **Math:** comparing multiple perspectives in problem-solving (with others), seeing the social context of math, using mathematical thinking in things like Needs Assessments and surveys, incorporating an empathy perspective into word problems. This helps to humanize data and statistics.
- **Science:** seeing the social side of science, engaging in empathy-driven design solutions in STEM, exploring the human side of scientific phenomena, dealing with bias in science, being inclusive in sharing examples from science
- **Social Studies:** empathy-driven service learning opportunities, exploring multiple perspectives and multiple histories, examining areas in history with false empathy
- **Reading:** using stories to build empathy, introducing students to other ideas and cultures, addressing injustice in literature, integrating informational reading into empathy-driven design challenges
- **Writing:** building empathy with an audience, using shared writing as a way to build empathy with multiple students, using writing to explore questions that might develop empathy

- **Health / Physical Education:** using empathy as a way to explore positive body image, focusing on empathy within inclusion in sports, exploring examples of empathy within sports and fitness, solving health-related problems through empathy-based design
- **Foreign Language:** using foreign languages as a way to build understanding with people of various cultures, exploring how the experience of learning a new language might lead to empathy toward people learning English, creating a design challenge that focuses on empathy between cultures
- **Music:** exploring how music makes people feel and using it to develop empathy, analyzing music from multiple countries and cultures as a vehicle for empathy, composing music with empathy toward an audience
- **Art:** creating works of art with empathy at the forefront. This might involve a work of art that develops empathy *in* the audience or it might be a specific work of art created from a place of empathy *with* an audience.

EMPATHY IN ACTION

In a previous chapter, I mentioned Melissa Deutsch. One year, her students spent three weeks on a history board game project. They engaged in research and talked to experts. They watched videos and read articles online.

However, one of the most powerful elements was empathy. From the start of their design, they knew that they would be sending their board games to local coffee shops.

She describes it this way, "A key part of the project-based approach, and one that is often skipped over, is presenting to an authentic audience. An audience beyond the students' classroom peers. Teachers often feel like this takes too much time and effort. But I encourage them to approach it in a different way. An audience doesn't have to be a room full of parents or a field trip to the local library or senior center. It just needs to be seen or heard beyond the walls of the classroom."

Eventually, they launched their projects and sought out user feedback. They would watch people play the games and ask for advice on how to iterate. In the process, they gained new perspectives on accessibility, culture, and language.

There are countless teachers implementing empathy-driven design thinking projects with their students. Students are creating works for nursing homes, veterans' hospitals, and refugee organizations. They are connecting with marginalized members of their local community. In the process, they are improving their creative work and learning the content at a deeper level. But it's not just about creativity. The longer impact of empathy is a service to humanity.

TRY THIS:
STRUCTURES FOR EMPATHY

Vintage Innovation Resources

If you want to get started with empathy-driven design, check out the five empathy structures you can use within a design thinking project. You can find these in the Vintage Innovation Toolkit at vintageinnovationbook.com/toolkit.

CHAPTER 8

IN A WORLD OF SOCIAL MEDIA, OUR STUDENTS NEED TO BE

CITIZEN JOURNALISTS

A few years ago, my daughter asked, "Dad, were you alive back when people had flip phones?" Another time, my son asked his substitute teacher why he had a burn phone. I had to explain, "He wasn't a drug dealer. Some people actually prefer flip phones." That's right, the cutting-edge cell phone I had in college is now considered a burner phone. Meanwhile, my other son "discovered" Crossy Road. Instantly, I recognized it as an iteration on Frogger . . . which we used to play on a large box-like system. When I was a kid, I always had to doublecheck if the television was supposed to be on channel two or channel three. Now, a whole host of games are available on a tablet with the tap of a button.

I never anticipated having to ask my sons, "Is it just you or are your friends here, too?" when entering the living room and seeing them playing a video game. On several occasions, I busted out into song and dance only to have my middle son quietly remind me that he was in a 12-person party and they could all hear me singing Fleetwood Mac's "The Chain." For what it's worth, I think I nailed the song. I can do a pretty good Stevie Nicks. Just kidding. I sound terrible.

As a professor, I now teach a generation of university students who were too young to remember a world without touchscreens or friend counts or instant media at their fingertips. We often miss the seismic change of social media because it's so invisible and pervasive. We cruise Facebook when we're bored without asking if boredom might be a valuable element to creative thinking. We share our photos on Instagram without asking what we miss if we're not living in the moment.

"WERE YOU ALIVE BACK WHEN PEOPLE HAD FLIP PHONES?"

– MY DAUGHTER –

But we also fail to appreciate the positive aspects of our technology. It's pretty amazing that I can ask a question and then take a deep dive into Wikipedia to find tons of answers. And, while technology can be distracting, it was a life-saver for a year when I lived away from my family. Although I was able to travel back to Phoenix for a week each month, I looked forward to our weekly family dinners via Google Hangouts and the daily texts they sent me from the home phone.

A WORLD OF SOCIAL MEDIA

We inhabit a world of social media, where our tools are also our spaces.

You can see it in the language people use. When someone says, "I don't know how to use Snapchat," they're viewing it as a tool but when someone says, "I was on Facebook for three hours last night," they view it as a space. This fusion of space and tool continues to change the way we relate. For example, it's normal for publishing platforms to have metrics attached to circulation and popularity. However, we now apply these metrics to social interactions for the first time in human history due to social media.

Imagine making a list of all your friends and placing the number on your doorway. That would be admittedly weird. Picture yourself at a party and telling a joke and then asking people to give you a thumbs up if they liked it, then counting the number and walking into a room and announcing the number to everyone willing to listen. That's essentially how Facebook works.

We grapple with these changes as we try to define ourselves and our social relationships in an era of constant connectivity. A few decades ago, if someone claimed to have "followers" you'd assume he or she was starting a cult. Now it's a phrase that 12-year-olds use when they talk about Instagram and Twitter. As a middle school teacher, I saw the dark side of social media metrics, as students would show up to class in tears because not enough people had liked their Instagram posts. I witnessed some of the ugliest cruelty of cyberbullying.

According to a Stanford study, only 25% of high school students were able to identify an accurate news story when also given a fake one.[70] Students also had a hard time distinguishing between real and fake photographs as well as authentic and staged videos. Researchers used the words "bleak" and "dismaying" to describe it. But it's not going away anytime soon and that's a very real problem.

It's tempting in these moments to ask students to avoid social media entirely. But what if the answer isn't avoidance but rather engagement? What if we taught students to document their world and share what mattered to them? What if we taught them to not only think critically about the information they consume but to also contribute something positive as well?

For all the darkness that exists online, I've seen students use social media to improve the world. I've seen them organize thank you events for staff and teachers. I've seen them video conference with authors and content experts. I've seen them design campaigns for positive social change in their own city.

Consider Bill Ferriter, a sixth-grade science teacher in North Carolina. When learning about the health and the human body system, students began exploring the role of sugar as a major public health crisis. What began with curiosity led to research and ultimately a grassroots campaign.

They launched the #sugarkills blog[71], writing about the pervasive ways that sugar consumption was impacting their local community and what that means for the larger global society. It was a truly vintage innovation approach, mixing face to face experiences with online journalism. It was a modern application of a vintage idea: citizen journalism.

WHAT IS CITIZEN JOURNALISM?

It's easier than ever to publish to the world. At one time, you needed a radio tower, recording equipment and permission from the authorities to publish audio to a mass market. Now, you need a device and an RSS feed. Video cameras once cost thousands of dollars and editing was laborious and expensive. Now, you can record on your phone and upload to social media. You no longer need a printing press to share the latest news. Simply press publish on a blog and your post is available to the world.

WHEN STUDENTS MAKE SENSE
OUT OF THEIR WORLD,
THEY BECOME THE ONES WHO
TRANSFORM IT.

It's no surprise, then, that you've seen a movement toward citizen journalism, where people document the events happening in their world. However, while the term emerged in the early 1990's,[72] it's actually a deeply vintage idea.

In the U.S., most early colonial newspapers were small outlets, without formal professional journalists. Instead, journalists were citizens employed in other fields who wanted to capture the news and share it with their community. Historian Frank Luther Mott describes it this way, "Thus, the editor is to be thought of chiefly as an entrepreneur. He had other affairs besides his newspaper on his hands. He was a job-printer and usually a publisher of books and pamphlets." [73] There was a DIY element to early journalism.

Unfortunately, there was a dark side to this citizen journalism. Wild conspiracies sometimes spread from city to city due to irresponsible citizen journalists. Early citizens used the press to spread bigotry and hatred and defend slavery. Marginalized groups, including ethnic minorities, women, and religious minorities rarely had access to the printing presses. But for all its flaws, the free press was also a tool for liberty and liberation, especially for the early abolitionist movements that were deemed too radical for the mainstream.

We now live in a new era of citizen journalism, where the lines are blurred between social spaces and publishing platforms. It's easier than ever to spread misinformation and craft fake news. We are active participants in the journalistic process every time we click "share" or "like." However, this reality shouldn't steer us away from citizen journalism. Instead, we should teach students how to be responsible citizen journalists documenting their world.

MY JOURNALISM JOURNEY

If you looked at my teaching contracts, it would appear that I taught journalism for three of my twelve teaching years. But that's not entirely accurate. While I formally taught social studies and later self-contained (all subjects), I always taught journalism.

It started in my first year of teaching when we were assigned intervention periods. Nobody else on my team wanted to teach writing intervention . . . which felt like a mistake, because writing is one of my favorite subjects to teach.

However, I quickly realized that my students HATED writing. So, I began with the question, "How do you feel about writing?" They described the boredom, the anger, and the frustration of writing. They hated writing prompts and wanted the freedom to choose their own topics. They hated the formulaic nature of the editing process. They hated the fact that they were writing to the teacher.

I realized that they didn't hate writing. They hated fake writing. They hated artificial prompts. They hated waiting two weeks for feedback, knowing that they had submitted to an audience of one.

So, I pitched an idea. "We are going to run an online magazine. We can do articles and audio articles." I'm not even sure the term "podcast" existed yet but if it did, I wasn't aware of it.

At first, my students hated it. They grumbled. They whined. They told me that it wasn't fun. A few of them preferred the dry, predictable worksheets that had used in a previous intervention class.

However, something changed a few weeks later when they saw their work online. Over the next month, the class culture changed as they began to take more ownership in the learning.

Later in the year, I did a documentary project with students and we combined the videos, podcasts, with the articles from the intervention class to create an online magazine. Students named it Social Voice. Two of the students sketched out a logo:

It felt edgy and different and . . . well . . . not very school-ish. Students created the tagline. "Our voice to our world." And it became more than a tagline. It became a purpose and a mission.

Social Voice quickly spilled over into my regular social studies class, where students began filming documentaries (a project we had piloted in the previous semester) and recording podcasts. This same year, I piloted a PBL approach and added elements of design thinking as a way to start with empathy as we started adding service projects and murals. But at its core, this was citizen journalism.

WHAT DO STUDENTS ACTUALLY NEED?

When people talk about the future of learning, they often mention technology and engineering. You hear about robotics classes and coding projects. While I love the emphasis on STEM and STEAM, I can't help but wonder if we forget about journalism because it isn't shiny and new.

And yet, if you ask people what type of technology skills students will need in the future, you'll hear things like digital citizenship, media literacy, and creative thinking. Unfortunately, schools tend to teach these topics in isolation, as if they exist in separate little buckets.

But journalism takes the buckets and mixes them all together. Here, these ideas overlap constantly.

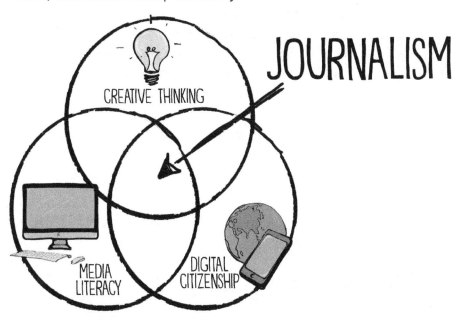

Journalism integrates digital citizenship, media literacy, and creativity in a connective and authentic way. Instead of teaching mini-lessons on these topics, students discover these ideas as they engage in inquiry, research, content creation, and publishing. Here's what I mean:

DIGITAL CITIZENSHIP

It's easy to approach digital citizenship with a fear-based mindset. I've had times when I send students the message of, "you better not screw this thing up, kids." I crafted lessons on the dangers of digital footprints, the importance of being nice, and the need to follow the rules.

But is that really citizenship? Don't we want our students to grow into critical thinking citizens who change the world? Don't we want them to learn what it means to engage in hard conversations while still being kind and empathetic? Don't we want them to advocate for things that they care about?

Those ideas are at the forefront of digital journalism. It's the belief that students should engage with the world in meaningful ways. Sometimes it means sharing their passions and interests with the world. Other times, it's means advocating for issues that they care about. But the common idea is the notion of a citizen journalist who thinks critically about their world. Here, students learn to leverage the creative and connective power of their technology.

MEDIA LITERACY AND INFORMATION LITERACY

Journalism takes media literacy a step further than merely critical reading. True, students learn how to read critically but they also need to learn how to construct critically. They internalize the mindset of critical reading as they create content that is trustworthy by identifying credible sources, analyzing the bias of sources, and comparing information from multiple credible sources.

If you think about basketball, it's a complex game with all kinds of offensive and defensive schemes. You can study it as a fan but you understand the mindset and the inner workings of the game when you play it yourself. Similarly, you can appreciate art at a deep level as a scholar but there's something powerful about this understanding when you sit before a canvas on your own. It's both humbling and empowering.

The same is true of students who engage in journalism. When they craft their own articles, podcasts, and videos, they gain a better understanding of how media works.

 # CREATIVE THINKING

I am passionate about seeing students develop a maker mindset, but often when we hear the term "maker," we think of engineering. Students prototyping with 3D printers and CAD machines. But there's another side of the maker mindset that is rooted in context. It's what happens when students engage in inquiry and problem-solving by looking at things from multiple perspectives, craft a work with intentionality, and share their work to an authentic audience.

These creative elements are central to journalism, as students move from inquiry through research, into iterative thinking, and eventually into the creation and launch of multimedia content.

When students own the entire publishing process, they think creatively and develop a maker mindset. They find their creative voice.

BUT ISN'T JOURNALISM A DYING INDUSTRY?

It can sound crazy to open an elementary or middle school journalism program when local newspapers are going out of business. Why prepare students for a job that will no longer exist? However, I'd argue that the industry isn't dying so much as evolving. Look at the sheer number of professional bloggers, podcasters, and video bloggers (vloggers). It's a massive industry. True, many of them aren't journalists in the traditional sense. Some of them spread misinformation. But doesn't that actually speak to the necessity of learning how to think like a journalist? Whether you are a foodie blogger or you're doing a political podcast, there is value in learning how to investigate, research, think critically, and communicate clearly.

But I wonder if the "Isn't the industry dying?" question misses the point. After all, we still teach P.E. despite the fact that most kids will not become professional athletes. We still teach music even when cities are cutting their symphony and opera programs. We teach math, even though few students will grow up to be professional mathematicians. We have chess clubs and competitions despite the fact that none of the students will grow up to become kings or queens ordering medieval knights to attack unsuspecting villages. We do these things because they help students learn how to think differently and live differently. Similarly, journalism matters because we all benefit asks students to make sense out of their world as critical thinking citizens.

JOURNALISM IS EVERYWHERE

Journalism isn't limited to language arts or social studies. Every time a student shares an idea, a process, or a story, they're engaging in citizen journalism. When I taught eighth grade, my students had a blog called Math in Real Life, where they interviewed professionals who shared how they used math in their contexts. Students created video tutorials for solving problems. They deconstructed poorly designed graphs that they found on the news. The message was clear: we're mathematical journalists.

TRY THIS:
DIGITAL JOURNALISM PROJECTS

Digital journalism is a vintage innovation approach that combines the timeless craft of journalism with newer digital technologies. If you want to get started with podcasting and blogging, download the free resources in the Vintage Innovation Toolkit at vintageinnovationbook.com/toolkit.

CHAPTER 9

IN A GLOBALIZED WORLD, OUR STUDENTS NEED TO EMRBACE THE

LOCAL

It was supposed to be the perfect project. My students would team up with students in three other cities around the world in a global citizenship project. They would work on collaborative teams to research a global issue and design a creative solution. I met with three other teachers via Skype. We shared our plans on a Google Document. I hyped it up with a preview video. I even dressed up in a costume. This would be epic.

Then it tanked.

Badly.

One school had an unexpected holiday while another school lost their internet for a day and another school had a sudden requirement to prepare for a state testing. Meanwhile, we had a lockdown. Not a lockdown drill, but an actual lockdown, with a gunman loose in the surrounding neighborhood. When my students finally met with their collaborative groups, we experienced some painful culture conflict between our low-income school and an affluent private school in another city.

For all the talk of a connected, globalized society, we learned the hard way that we could not ignore the power and pull of geography. Yes, students could use shared documents, but they would still be working in completely different time zones. True, they could transcend space, but they could not avoid the messy realities of cultural clashes that we, as teachers, had failed to address ahead of time.

That weekend, I met with the three other teachers and we came to a difficult conclusion: if we wanted them to be global citizens, they would need to focus on the local first. So, we retooled the project to focus on what globalization looked like in our own neighborhoods. My students began researching the history of the Maryvale area of Phoenix, including the larger question of what happened to the now-abandoned factories. They interviewed residents about the changes that had occurred as the larger chains had moved in and replaced neighborhood stores. Suddenly, they could see the deeply personal issue of immigration as a part of larger, globalized trends.

In the end, my students shared their findings with students in other countries. They began conversations via email where they learned about the transnational companies that existed in each location. My students were shocked to find that these other students read similar books, listened to similar music, and loved the same greasy Chicken McNuggets. Full disclosure: I, too, love McNuggets. You're not supposed to say that when you're a professor. You're supposed to be like, "no, I only eat organic quinoa." But I love McNuggets.

Eventually, we turned the research into videos and storyboards for a documentary we called *Maryvale Voice*. It wasn't just a story about globalization. It was *our* story of globalization. Along the way, I learned a valuable lesson: if I want students to become responsible global citizens, it needs to start in our backyard.

Note that my students embraced the vintage innovation idea of a mash-up. By filming a documentary, students embraced the technological while also engaging in personal, face-to-face conversations. By exploring the local community, they made sense out of larger global trends that they then communicated with a global audience.

 THE FUTURE IS LOCAL

When I talk to my friends in engineering, technology, and finance, they often describe working in collaborative teams that span the globe. For example, you might have a simultaneous conference call with members in India, France, and Jordan. It would

126

seem, then, that we need to get students working in multinational small groups to prepare them for these types of collaborative projects. And there's definitely some validity in these types of learning experiences. They can be powerful.

However, if we want students to value diversity and embrace the human connection, they need to embrace the diversity in their own communities. While technology can connect students globally, a personal conversation can expand their world. Although students can collaborate on a shared document, they can also learn to collaborate through a shared service learning experience.

Paradoxically, when students interact with and serve their local community, they learn the transferrable soft skills that will allow them to thrive in a globalized world.

SERVE YOUR LOCAL COMMUNITY

Trevor Muir was passionate about the plight of refugees who had fled natural disasters and war zones to forge a new life in the U.S. As a high school history teacher in Grand Rapids, Michigan, he wanted to share his heart for refugees with his students. Instead of simply sharing a short video or reading an article from a far-off land, he asked his students to open their eyes to the stories of the refugees in their own community.

On a cold Michigan morning, his students huddled around the front of the class and listened, eyes-wide, as Danysa shared her story. Trevor described it this way in *The Epic Classroom*,[74] "She talked about losing her entire family to violence twenty years ago in the Rwandan genocide. Danysa talked to my students about her husband being killed with a machete as she hid inside a hotel room at the *Hotel des Mille Collines*. You might have seen the movie. I did not have to tell any students in my class to put their cell phones away that morning. The room was silent, and all eyes were glued to the front of the room where a Rwandan woman used broken English to share her story."

Danysa described the confusion of navigating a new country. Although she had amazing resilience and problem-solving skills, she was overwhelmed by her new country. She once got on the bus and didn't know how to signal the stop to the bus driver and spent five hours travelling around the city hoping someone would help her. Trevor looked around at his class, tears streaming down their faces.

They were changing. His students were growing more empathetic, more compassionate, and more open-minded. Her story unlocked their ability to see an invisible community in their own neighborhoods.

But it didn't stop there. During the debrief, one student said, "This is stupid. How come no one showed her how to stop a bus? It's not that hard."

From there, Trevor led them through an inquiry and research process. They teamed up with a local agency with the goal of empathy-driven design, where they would design *with* rather than design *for*. Students met with teams of refugees, listening to their stories and hearing their pain points. Eventually, they created brochures, cookbooks, flashcards, and videos for a local social work agency that distributed the resources to new refugees. The students teamed up with members of the community who helped translate and ensure that the students were showing cultural humility.[75] Eventually, they launched their products to an authentic audience in the form of product presentations with the refugee agency. Along the way, they were learning how make sense out of unjust systems and advocate for change.

SOMETIMES, THE BEST WAY
TO LEARN GLOBAL CITIZENSHIP
IS TO SERVE THE
LOCAL COMMUNITY

In the end, they shared their ideas with a local organization. Trevor describes it this way, "The students put on their best outfits because they knew it was not a normal presentation; they were presenting to working professionals . . . Group after group, students made their way to the front of the room to show their fine-tuned products to our guests. My students acted like seasoned professionals themselves that day, and were more focused, serious, and engaged than I'd ever seen them before."

This project not only impacted the community, it changed the students' lives. They learned empathy, collaboration, communication, and critical thinking. They learned how to deal with the kind of cross-cultural conflict they would eventually face when doing global collaboration projects. Note, too, that even though it was a vintage idea (serve your local neighborhood) with a deeply human connection, they still used video editing software and smartphones. One student made an app that the agency loaded onto old smartphones. Another student learned the ins and outs of Photoshop. It was a vintage concept with modern tools.

THE VALUE OF SOFT SKILLS

I asked Trevor about how his students had changed from this experience and his list was nearly identical to what my students had experienced. Here's are some of the soft skills students develop as they engage locally.

Collaboration: They learn to collaborate in a face-to-face environment.

Work Ethic: They work harder. In my experience, students who serve their local community learn how to work hard for a goal.

Suddenly, they're sharing their product (whether it's a design product or a service activity) with an authentic audience.

Citizenship: They learn citizenship, not simply as an idea or a list of rules but as something deeply personal and profound.

Empathy: They gain empathy. When students engage in service learning, they learn how to listen to people's stories and pay attention to what others are going through.

New Perspectives: They have access to diverse perspectives. We tend to organize schools into rigid categories based on age and grade level. Often, we place students into additional tracks, where students from multiple mastery levels rarely interact with each other. But service learning projects are different. Here, they get the opportunity to meet people from diverse backgrounds.

Communication: They improve in their communication by engaging with people from other generations, life experiences, and cultures. They learn how to ask questions and listen.

Notice that all of these things are the skills our students will need to thrive in a globalized society. However, they learned these life-long skills through experiences where they had to be full present in the moment.

Moreover, these experiences make the subject come alive. Students see the subject as relevant to their world. Suddenly, math isn't simply an abstract exercise. Instead, it's rooted in their experiences and used by members of their community. History isn't something distant and far away. It's something we live and experience.

THEY LEARN HOW
TO COLLABORATE

THEY ARE EMPOWERED
TO CHANGE THE WORLD

THEY ASK DEEPER
QUESTIONS

WHEN STUDENTS
CONNECT WITH THE
LOCAL
COMMUNITY

THEY BUILD
PARTNERSHIPS

THEY IMPROVE
IN THEIR
COMMUNICATION

THEY DEVELOP
EMPATHY

THEY GAIN NEW
PERSPECTIVES

THEY BECOME BETTER
GLOBAL CITIZENS

THEY LEARN TO
LISTEN TO
FEEDBACK

THEY SEE THE
CONTENT AS
RELEVANT TO THEIR LIVES

THEY BECOME ADVOCATES
FOR WHAT THEY BELIEVE IN

THE LOCAL CONNECTION

So, how do we help our students connect with the diversity of their own local community? Here are a few ideas.

Search for guest speakers: While face-to-face approaches work well, students can also go out into the community and record conversations using smart phones or other devices.

Try a "show and tell" approach to homework. We tend to assign homework that asks students to take schoolwork into their world. Often, students fail to turn in their work. But what if it's shows and tell? Suddenly, kids can't wait to bring in an item from their world and share it with the class. Show and tell is essentially the opposite of homework. It's a chance for students to bring their world into the school rather than school into their world. This approach honors student agency. When I taught eighth grade, I encouraged a "show and tell" approach to homework. Here, they could bring in experts, resources, videos, or audio from their own community as they worked on projects in class. It was always optional but many students choose to complete it, since it was a chance to bring their world into class.

Seek out partnerships. Real partnerships involve seeking expertise and opinions from the community. They involve asking students to serve the community. We once did a graffiti removal project using the design thinking process. Students pitched their ideas to our principal, a few community organizers, a few parents, and some local business leaders. The winning design project was a mural project that ended up preventing graffiti while also beautifying the neighborhood.

Find the community context for your subject. Ask where you see the foreign language, physical movement, art, music, math, science, history, and publishing in your local community. Then find ways to connect the lessons to that immediate context. Students might blog about their cultural holidays or traditions in a world cultures class. They might interview family members to tap into their own stories in a social studies class. Students can also capture the history in their own neighborhood through video and audio or explore a natural phenomenon (something we'll be exploring in the next chapter) in their own neighborhoods. They might conduct needs assessments and surveys for math or they might create videos and tutorials on their outside hobbies when writing functional texts in language arts.

Look for places to serve. While it's important to connect with the community, students will ultimately learn more when they actually serve their community as well. We can incorporate service learning[76] into all subjects or even take a multiple subject approach so students see the connections between disciplines, ideas, and contexts.

A VINTAGE INNOVATION APPROACH TO APPRENTICESHIPS

Russ Goerend is an award-winning innovative educator who helped pilot the Waukee Apex program[77]. Borrowing from the vintage idea of an apprenticeship, his students would connect with the local community to help solve problems.

However, this program is more like an apprenticeship in reverse. Instead of leaving school each day to work in the community, they bring the community into their school. Local businesses come to the school asking for help. They're created PSAs for the minor league baseball team, made websites for local health care organizations, and done mini-projects for non-profits.

Notice that his students are adding a modern twist to a vintage idea. They're using studios, 3D printers, and computers to work on their projects. But at the heart is a very vintage idea: serving your neighbor.

Goerend's students spend the first few weeks in an onboarding process, where they learn how to communicate professionally and collaborate with community members. From there, they engage in an inquiry-based, project-based approach to content creation. Although the approach is cutting edge, the community-oriented approach harkens back to Dewey.

In the end, his students are learning all kinds of skills that they will use as they enter a globalized workforce. By working locally, they have collaborated with diverse populations and gained new perspectives. They've solved problems by focusing on empathy. In the process, they are becoming creative, critical thinking citizens – not just of the world but of *their* world.

CHAPTER 10

IN A WORLD OF VIRTUAL REALITY, OUR STUDENTS NEED TO STUDY

NATURE

We gather outside on a worn-out blanket strewn over the hot the cul-de-sac pavement. No handouts. No close reading exercises. Just a bunch of families in the neighborhood breaking bread, eating bacon, and talking about life – except the lone vegan in our group. She skipped out on the bacon.

The morning progresses with small talk and banter and impromptu games of catch. Occasionally, we put on our dark solar eclipse glasses and glance at the slight circle forming covering part of the sun. Eventually, the shadows change. The light grows dimmer as we make finger puppets that feel out of this world. And yet, it remains uneventful.

Finally, it starts feeling real. For the next few minutes, we watch as the world feels slightly sepia-toned. My wife and kids gather close as the countdown begins.

All at once, it happens. The stars appear and the temperature drops. Unreal. I stare out at the total eclipse, the bright white circle enveloping the sky. It's breath-taking. It's beautiful.

I squeeze my wife's hand. We know we are witnessing something magical. But the real magic isn't just eclipse. It's the look on our kids' faces, consumed with awe and wonder— a certain kind that can only occur when we are truly able to observe the beauty of our universe.

OUR VIRTUAL WORLD

We live in an increasingly virtual world, with a barrage of text and moving images and noise at the click of a button. I can binge-watch my favorite shows and instantly access my favorite music. I can tap an icon and talk with friends all over the world. Anytime. Anywhere. We inhabit these virtual spaces, the abstract third space between two locations, without giving it much thought. Instinctively, when I'm bored, I flip on the Twitter app. If I'm a passenger in a car, I nearly always check if there's a Pokémon hanging out nearby. It's become so normal it almost feels invisible.

Meanwhile, things continue to change. Last year, I got a virtual reality headset for my birthday and it was amazing. I rode a pretend roller coaster nineteen times. Did I need to? Probably not. Did I do it? Absolutely. Another time, I watched a 3D basketball game and I swear it felt like I was in the arena watching my Golden State Warriors route the Sacramento Kings. It was amazing – the headset and not the game. The game was pretty much what I expected from the Warriors in a year when they still dominated the NBA.

I found myself saying, "We need more of this at school. We need to figure out how to leverage VR for virtual field trips and dissections and other immersive experiences."

And yet . . . we also need more nature. We need more awe and wonder. We need more eclipse moments to jar us from our virtual world and remind us what really matters. Our devices compress the world, making it easier to connect. But nature does the opposite. It gives us space and humbles us.

WHY NATURAL WONDERS MAKE US MORE CREATIVE

Wonder is powerful in itself. We shouldn't need to ask, "how is this useful?" when taking the time to go for a walk or observe a sunset. We need nature simply because we need wonder and awe and beauty and joy.

However, there is also a transformative element to nature that makes us more creative. If you ask some of the most innovative artists, engineers, and entrepreneurs, you might be surprised by how often they go hiking or take long walks. There's something powerful about slowing down and taking in the beauty of our universe. These moments actually increase divergent thinking and improve our ability to problem-solve.[78]

And yet . . the natural world can feel like a luxury for teachers. We inhabit a world of buzzing fluorescent lights and industrial carpet. We deal with the incessant pressures of the standardized tests and the push to make kids future-ready. Gardens and nature walks can feel hippity-dippity. Like, "that's a cute idea but I actually have a curriculum map I need to follow."

However, natural wonder has a practical element. It boosts student curiosity and increases creativity. Here's why.

Nature creates positive disruptions. Going out into nature will pull us from rhythm of industrial life and from the narrow algorithm-based worldview of our echo chambers. This morning as I went hiking, I was suddenly whisked away from the cacophony of current events and latest education fads in my Twitter feed and immersed in the natural beauty of the Oregon forest. This had a re-centering affect that actually allowed me to think more creatively when I arrived home.

Nature encourages problem-solving. Ever noticed that some of your best ideas happen while you are taking a shower, sitting in the car, or going for a walk? There's a reason for this. In *Rest,* Alex Soojung-Kim Pang explores how some of the greatest thinkers use long walks as ways to think deeply about seemingly unrelated ideas.[79] For example, Charles Darwin used to go on long walks in the country and play around with the ideas of his evolutionary theory. While we often think of this time as a luxury, this was more like a daily discipline that allowed his mind to process information by connecting seemingly disconnected ideas.

Nature helps us embrace deep work. There's an interesting research study from the University of Michigan. Students were asked to take a long walk before engaging in a concentration activity. The first group went out into a wooded area while the second group walked through the bustling city center. The first group not only scored better in a deep work activity but their results continued a full week later. The bottom line? When we go into nature, we are able to do focused work afterward. And that, right there, is vital for creative work.[80]

Nature humbles us while also expanding our worldview. I have a smartphone that allows me to connect to the world instantaneously. But when I explore the natural world, I see that the world cannot be compressed, shrink-wrapped, and shipped. Yes, our devices are connected, but we still need to break bread and eat bacon and laugh and tell stories and wander around the forest. This has a humbling effect while also expanding our worldview. And when this happens, our creative work is able to expand.

Nature can spark innovation. When you think about the future of space travel, you don't usually think of geckos. And yet, NASA is studying these lizards to try and understand how to create better adhesives.[81] [82] The natural world is often the inspiration for innovation. We'll be getting deeper into this idea later in this chapter.

If we want our students to grow into creative thinkers, we need to move beyond the makerspace (and please note that I'm a huge fan of makerspaces) and out into the natural world. That 3D printer is awesome but picking the first strawberries from a garden can feel magical. With my trusty Macbook, I feel like I can do just about anything but a forest will nearly always remind me of my own limitations.

A MAKERSPACE IS GREAT BUT SO IS A GARDEN

THE POWER OF BIOMIMICRY

For years, Europeans printed texts on old rags soaked in urine. That's right, some of our best ancient manuscripts are printed on pee pee paper. The Chinese had already perfected paper-making using bamboo and mulberry fibers. But in Europe and North America, pee pee paper remained the texture of choice.

However, in 1719, French scientist René Réaumur made an important connection while studying wasps. He noticed that they essentially created paper by chewing up and spitting out fragments of wood. What if humans did the same thing? I mean, we wouldn't literally have to eat wood and spit it up. That would be gross. But we could emulate parts of the process.

Réaumur didn't actually perfect the science of modern paper-making. But his question lingered around until others began experimenting with designs. It took an entire century for the idea to catch on. People continued to use pee pee paper. But those who created our modern notion of paper continued to study wasp nests for inspiration.[83]

We see this often. Southwest Airlines studied ant colony behavior as they developed the choose-your-own-seat system.[84] [85] When Japanese bullet trains were creating ear splitting "tunnel booms," engineer and birdwatcher Eiji Nakatsu collaborated with a team of designers who created a mash-up design from three different bird species.[86] Engineers have studied shark skin, spider webs, and armadillos in developing new surfaces.

While we often think of nature as an inspiration for poetry and art, our natural world often serves as a source for inspiration in design and engineering. This is all part of a field of design called biomimetics, pioneered by the biologist Janine Benyus.[87] Here, engineers embrace the process of biomimicry, where they copy models, systems, and objects in the natural world as they solve problems. Sometimes, something in nature sparks a new idea and they apply it to a relevant problem. Other times, they take a pre-existing problem and look to nature to solve it.

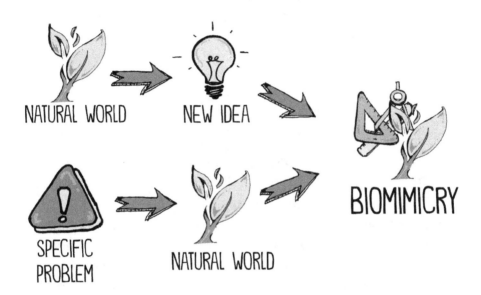

NATURAL WORLD   NEW IDEA

SPECIFIC
PROBLEM   NATURAL WORLD

BIOMIMICRY

RETHINKING STEM / STEAM

When we think of STEM and STEAM, we often connect engineering to physics or maybe even chemistry. Sometimes we dive into environmental science, with a push toward using human-created design to solve environmental issues. But biomimicry reminds us that innovation in design often works the opposite way, with nature helping us solve deeply human problems rather than using engineering to solve ecological problems.

So, what does this mean for teachers?

When I taught a STEM block, I rarely, if ever, considered the role of biomimicry in design. Although we looked at green design for our eco-friendly kitchen products, we never really considered how our biological ecosystem could influence the design process. I wish I had asked students to make connections between the systems within an ecosystem and the design challenges in our human-created systems. We often talk about the role of empathy and human connection within design thinking. But what if we asked students to explore both the physical characteristics and the behavior of the biological world?

OPTION #1
USE THE NATURAL WORLD AS A STARTING PLACE FOR OPEN-ENDED DESIGN.

When we first moved to Oregon, people said that all we would get is a "light dusting" of snow. But in late December, the "light dusting" was more like a dump of snow and our Phoenix-raised kids had their first ever snow days. They played around with it, building snow men, snow women, and, of course, snow unicorns – because . . . unicorns, why not?

At one point, my oldest son asked me, "Which chemical or substance will melt snow the fastest?"

His hypothesis was that salt would work the best. Still, he wanted to test it out. From there, he tested out vinegar and oil (which is basically salad dressing), rubbing alcohol, shampoo, salt, sugar, and pretty much everything else he could get his hands on. When he discovered that rubbing alcohol worked better than salt, he decided we should make a de-icer for our car windshield. I realize that's not an original idea, but it was groundbreaking to him. It wasn't an invention that would change the world but it was something that changed his world.

This was a small example of using a design process that began, not with a scenario or a problem or even empathy with an audience, but with a sense of wonder and curiosity about the natural world. It started with playful observations, which led to questions, which led to experiments, and eventually ideation, and design.

Nature has a way of creating positive disruptions by pulling us out of our interests, ideas, and systems and into something that is often humbling. This is what happens when kids go into the forest or walk beside the beach. But it's also what happens when kids get to work in a garden.

As a teacher, you can ask questions like, "What fascinates you?" and "What does this make you wonder?" From there, students enter that place of curiosity and experimentation that often leads to inspiration and design. They start to pay attention to how the world works and over time, it inspires them to create something new. Note that this isn't meant to be a rigid system. Sometimes they don't end up designing anything new – and that's okay.

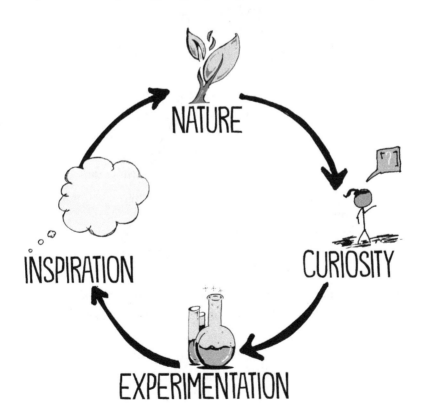

Notice, too, that this project didn't happen on accident. My son had a sixth-grade science teacher who embodied the vintage innovation mindset. Each semester, they worked on independent inquiry projects to answer their burning questions. Even the phrasing "which chemical or substance" revealed a connection between the scientific concepts and the world around him.

This approach has its limitations. It tends to be serendipitous, which can be a challenge when you have a highly-structured curriculum map with tight deadlines. There's also no guarantee that curiosity will always lead to experimentation or that experiments will always lead to design. However, there's another approach that uses biomimicry as a part of the research process rather than the starting point for design.

OPTION #2
INTEGRATE BIOMIMICRY INTO THE RESEARCH PROCESS.

A few years ago, I worked with Chris Kesler (a STEM curriculum expert) and A.J. Juliani on a set of STEM projects. One of my favorite projects involved students looking at various bird beaks in order to solve an engineering challenge. It was the first time I had seen the connection between adaptations, natural selection, and engineering. At first, I wondered if this was truly a STEM activity at all. Do engineers really think this way?

However, over the year, I've been interacting with more engineers at my university. At first, I assumed biomimicry was a small niche within the engineering community, but to my surprise, I found that engineers are often observing natural phenomenon in order to research potential solutions. One engineer described how he studied trees in order to rethink bridge design. Another described studying patterns in insect behavior when trying to make sense out of information architecture.

On some level, this requires advanced knowledge of both the engineering process and biology. However, teachers can help facilitate this type of thinking. If students are working on a specific engineering challenge, the teacher can provide curated resources that allow them to study the way organisms and ecosystems work in order to improve their designs.

SIX WAYS TO MAKE THIS A REALITY IN SCHOOLS

As a middle school teacher, I knew that nature was important. However, I lived in a world of tight curriculum maps and an incessant pressure to pass the test. I never even considered the role of the natural world until my last two years in the classroom, when another teacher created a garden and my photojournalism students would ask to visit it. I realized that it wasn't a luxury. It was a necessity. The following are five ways to incorporate the natural world into our teaching.

#1
CREATE MORE ACCESS TO NATURAL SPACES.

If possible, find ways to get students outside more often. While makerspaces can inspire creativity, so can gardens. We need to create green spaces that inspire students to observe and ask questions. In a digital world of virtual reality, augmented reality, and instant access to information, there is something deeply relevant in learning to slow down and pay attention to the natural world.

#2
LET STUDENTS PLAY MORE OFTEN IN NATURAL SPACES.

The seemingly spontaneous questions about the natural world are often the result of deep, relaxed, unstructured time. In other words, they're the result of play. We'll be addressing the idea of play in another chapter. However, there is something deeply restorative in playing within a natural space.

#3
HELP STUDENTS LEARN HOW TO OBSERVE.

When I had to teach about adaptations, I brought in insects, crustaceans, and plants for students to observe. Instead of taking pictures, they had to sketch out what they saw. I was going full-blown vintage by preventing devices. I asked them to spend five minutes looking at the organism in front of them. They hated it at first. But eventually, something clicked. They noticed things they hadn't paid attention to before. Nearly every group had at least one big "aha" moment that couldn't have happened if they were snapping pictures.

#4
INTEGRATE NATURAL OBSERVATIONS INTO THE RESEARCH PROCESS.

When students work on design thinking and engineering products, consider finding ways for them to observe the natural world before they ideate or prototype.

#5
ENCOURAGE STUDENTS TO ASK QUESTIONS ABOUT THE NATURAL WORLD.

Find opportunities for students to engage in self-directed, sustained inquiry about ecosystems and organisms and let them chase their curiosity. We'll be diving into inquiry-based learning in a future chapter. But this is the idea that students should ask questions about their natural world.

#6
CONNECT THE NATURAL WORLD TO ALL SUBJECTS.

Help students see the math that exists in the natural world, including patterns, shapes, and systems. If possible, find ways that they can see data in the natural world. Connect natural geography to history, so they have a deep concept of how context shapes events. Find connections between literature and the natural world. Let them see the patterns and geometry present in the natural world.

CREATING SPACES OF NATURAL WONDER

A few months ago, I visited a school in Australia with a high-tech makerspace. Students pulled out their laptops and worked on digital 3D models. They crafted blog posts and filmed videos in front of a greenscreen.

But when they got stuck, they walked away from the technology and wandered through a beautiful garden. During an inquiry-based science lesson, they moved seamlessly from watching a video on their iPads to studying the same phenomenon outside. A small group of students switched stations from a Scratch project to garden time. It was a reminder that vintage innovation is both/and. These students were equally excited about coding and gardening.

Although this looked messy and fun and playful, it was, on another level, serious business. The teachers were architects who had spent hours designing the systems and creating this space of vintage innovation. They studied the standards and found ways to connect informational text, videos, and gardens to the science standards. To the kids, it felt normal. It was fun. But the teachers knew that something profound was happening. Their students were more curious and more creative because of this sense of wonder.

TRY THIS:
NATURE-CENTERED LESSON

You might not have the time or the resources to create a garden – and that's okay. However, you can try developing a lesson that connects to the natural world. For ideas in your subject area, check out the free resource in the Vintage Innovation Toolkit at vintageinnovationbook.com/toolkit.

CHAPTER 11

IN A WORLD OF
AUGMENTED REALITY,
OUR STUDENTS NEED

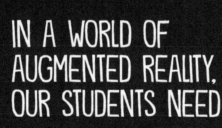

When I go home, I'm no longer a dad. I transform into a side-kick to the world's coolest superhero. I become a nurse to a stuffed animal surgeon. I get to help an architect and a builder of forts made from couch cushions and blankets. I become second-in-command on a pirate ship made of duct tape and cardboard. I morph into a lab assistant to an always-curious scientist. I turn into an astronaut in a planet in our backyard. I become a patron at an arcade testing out three new pinball machines made from random objects in our house.

That's the power of imagination.

It's an escape, yes, but it's a different kind of escape. It's not an escape *from* reality. It's an escape *back to* reality. It's a chance to recover what is lost when I defined myself in narrow terms as a teacher and a professional. I'm more consumed by wonder. I'm more curious. I'm more likely to explore questions that fascinate me even if they aren't "practical."

For the last fifteen years, I have found myself falling in love with subjects I had become convinced that I didn't like. I have rediscovered the wonder of scientific experiments and math manipulation. I want my kids to retain this sense of wonder. I want them to remain imaginative. I want them to follow curiosity and see where it leads. I want them to design and build and create and invent. I want them to play with ideas.

I realize that imagination changes over time. But it shouldn't be something that shrinks or diminishes. It should be something that expands and evolves. Maybe it gets more realistic. Maybe it grows more rooted in reality. But the imagination should expand over time. It turns out this sense of imagination is vital for the future. In a digital, programmed, augmented reality world, our students will need to imagine new possibilities.[88] If we want our students to become makers, inventors, artists, and engineers, they will need to retain this sense of imagination. They will need to dream up the impossible and then ask, "why not?"

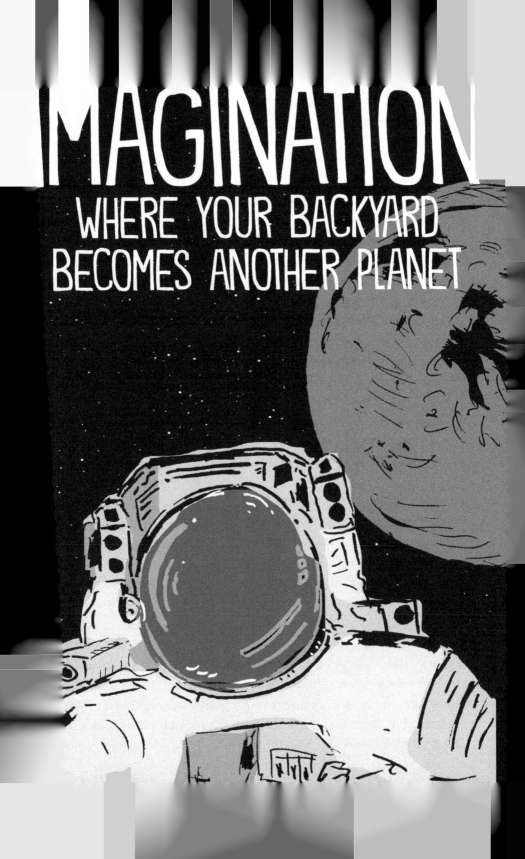

IMAGINATION MATTERS

This sense of imagination is vital for every single industry. I once made the mistake of telling my accountant friend, "I couldn't do what you do. I need a job that allows for more creativity."

He laughed and replied, "John, what do you think it takes to be a great accountant? We're problem-solvers. We're creative. The biggest mistakes in accounting are often a failure of imagination."

"Are you just saying accountants make up the rules?"

"Not at all. We have to stick to the rules but we are constantly generating new ideas within the tight parameters. The best people in finance can look at a complex situation and solve it in a way that shocks you. That kind of problem-solving takes imagination. I know that's a funny word to use here but that's what it is. It's imagination."

IMAGINATION AND THE FUTURE

Our world is changing. Social media means we live with one foot in the digital world and one foot in the physical world. Virtual reality is just beginning to reach viability, along with augmented reality and artificial intelligence.

None of those trends scare me. In fact, they excite me. Right now, I am minutes away from moving to Level 40 as a trainer in Pokémon Go. When I visit a new country one of my first questions is, "Do they have any regional Pokémon?" I'm a bona fide nerd.

And yet . . . when technology frequently augments our reality, we sometimes allow it to do the imaginative heavy lifting for us. In these moments, we inhabit pre-programmed multimedia land-scapes that limit our opportunity for imagination. This doesn't mean that technology inhibits creativity. Jane McGonigal points out that video games can improve problem-solving, collaboration, and goal-setting.[89] The rush of dopamine can actually improve performance and hard-work.

But there's a cost to the constant multimedia landscape.

Imagination needs time and space to grow. It needs minimalism and mind-wandering. Researcher Patricia Greenfield points out that reading on the internet trains us to scan information quickly and efficiently and digital tools can help improve visual-spatial.[90] However, frequent screen time can reduce "deep processing" that leads to "mindful knowledge acquisition, inductive analysis, critical thinking, imagination, and reflection."

My favorite augmented reality is a novel. I love getting lost in a fantastical world. For what it's worth, I'm still waiting for my owl to arrive and invite me to Hogwarts. I've cried when characters I loved died.

Sometimes the best way to be relevant is to step away from the digital and virtual and abstract and embrace the tangible and tactile and to augment your reality with nothing more than your imagination. Consider the vintage act of reading. Although reading can seem like a "consumer" activity, it is deeply imaginative and creative. When children spend hours reading, they are also spending hours imagining – which, over time, develop into the skills and habits they will need for a lifetime.

But there's another powerful way to spark imagination. It's something kids do naturally and it's an idea that's been around for millennia: play.

 THE POWER OF PLAY

Imagination is closely related to divergent thinking. However, according to a longitudinal study, 90% of kindergartners rank in the "genius" level for divergent thinking. Within five years, the number drops to 50% and has a steep decline afterward.[91] While some of this might be the result of human development, I think there's something else at work. Divergent thinking thrives when people play. There's a fascinating link between playfulness and divergent thinking.[92] Play allows for looser, more flexible thinking, which, in turn, helps people engage in divergent thinking. The researchers defined this as "physical, social and cognitive spontaneity; manifest joy; and sense of humor."

While this is obvious with children, playfulness turns out to be an attribute of the most productive creative teams. It turns out humor and joy (both tightly related to playfulness) are contributing factors to effective collaboration. When Google launched their Project Aristotle to study the attributes of the most effective teams, they found that psychological safety was critical and that the best teams were able to "play" with ideas and concepts.

As a teacher, I found that play often imaginative play often sparked a sense of wonder, which led to experimentation, and ultimately creativity. This cycle was natural and fluid. The goal was never, "I want to be more creative." Instead, it was simply, "I want to play." But that initial spark would lead to a deep sense of wonder, experimentation, and creativity, which led to deeper play as the cycle continued.

Although we need longer periods of open-ended play, we also feel the constraints of curriculum maps and school schedules. One way to incorporate a sense of play and imagination is through a low-tech game or simulation.

 # HANDS-ON GAMES

Two students in my social studies pedagogy class took on the challenge of designing a lesson to spark student wonder. They chose an area that they knew students would find confusing and maybe even a little boring: ancient China, trade, and the geopolitical structure. They knew that most sixth-grade students would lack both prior knowledge and intrinsic motivation to learn this topic. In other words, you don't see kids flocking to the library to check out a book on ancient Chinese trade practices.

Instead of starting with an informational text or a lecture to build prior knowledge, this pair started with a simulation. They divided the class up into small groups and passed out cards with trade items. Then, at each round, groups rolled dice to determine their potential yields on natural resources, followed by a chance to trade with other groups. But there was a catch: the teacher, representing China, determined the cost of silk.

In the end, we had a firm understanding of the role of luck in natural resources, the bitterness that can happen between nations, the role of trade, and the way that a nation could use trade to influence other nation's policies.

WHAT IS GAME-BASED LEARNING?

Game-based learning is an immersive experience, where students master learning targets through gameplay. Unlike a review game, game-based learning introduces new ideas and concepts through a virtual environment. The key thing here is that the learning happens *through* the game rather than *before* the game. Often, these games take on the form of a simulation that might involve world-building and character development.

When I taught social studies, we often used game-based simulations to process complex ideas. Students engaged in a communist, capitalist, and socialist version of Monopoly and took surveys to see whether they attributed wealth or poverty to luck or decision-making. Ultimately, they took on roles as characters in a society that had to design a mixed economy. We played a modified version of Risk in order to understand how the alliance system, imperialism, and nationalism would contribute toward World War I (and how a single "small event" could launch a war). Here, we also looked at war poetry comparing the Great War to cricket matches and contrasted that to the sheer destruction of World War I. We turned the class into a factory and created an urban planning game to learn about industrialization.

Greg Costikyan breaks gameplay down into the following components:[93] [94]

Interaction: the game changes with the players actions (and often with the players' interdependent actions)

Goal: there is a purpose to the game (and often this includes a winner or loser)

Struggle: every game has an element of a struggle, even if it's a non-competitive game (think Minecraft or Sim City, where the struggle is often creative)

Structure: games have rules, procedures, and systems

Endogenous Meaning: here the game structure creates its own meaning

ABSTRACT CONCRETE

CREATES A
BRIDGE BETWEEN THE
ABSTRACT AND CONCRETE

THE INFORMATION
STICKS

BOOSTS
ENGAGEMENT

FACILITATES
CRITICAL THINKING

REASONS TO TRY OUT
GAME-BASED LEARNING

SPARKS THE
LOVE OF LEARNING

STUDENTS MAKE CONNECTIONS
BETWEEN IDEAS

IT BECOMES A
SAFE PLACE TO
MAKE MISTAKES

INFORMATION IS MORE
ACCESSIBLE

WHY GAMES LEAD TO DEEPER LEARNING

The following are seven benefits of game-based learning:

Game-based learning boosts engagement. They go beyond what Phillip Schlechty calls "strategic compliance"[95] (high attention but low commitment) and into a place where they have full buy-in and true engagement. Students get the opportunity to make decisions, pursue a goal, and check their own progress.[96]

The information sticks. Here, students experience higher retention of the content.[97] Often, the games become mental models that students go back to in order to make sense out of what they have learned. Also, the debrief experience connects an often emotional, memorable experience with the content in a way that leads to a deeper, more permanent understanding. [98]

Immersive games can help students make connections between concepts and ideas. They see learning as interconnected. Often, we teach content in silos, with clear objectives and direct instruction. However, with game-based learning, students discover the content in a way that is connective rather than linear. In my experience, games helped students develop conceptual understanding.

Game-based learning bridges the abstract and the concrete. Games are fully immersive. Participants maneuver within their physical environment to make sense of the information. It's a way to teach concepts and systems that might seem opaque and distant in a way that is visual and experiential. It was hard for my students to wrap their minds around economic systems or imperialism, but a simulation game helped them make the connection. In some cases, they take on specialized roles and build empathy by taking on the role of characters.[99]

Information is more accessible. With game-based learning, students at all levels can participate in the process. There's a low barrier of entry. As an educator, it's all too easy for me to expect students to have strong prior knowledge or a mastery of reading and writing. But with a game, students get the chance to discover the content on more of an even playing field.

Students engage in critical thinking. Students are making decisions that require the analysis and synthesis. Later, they can use the simulation to answer critical thinking questions.

Games can help lead to a love of learning. Games are fun. And when students engage in game-based learning they begin to fall in love with the subject and the content and the ideas. They realize that it is intrinsically rewarding to geek out on learning. And that takes them one step closer to being lifelong learners.

KEEP GAMES LOW-TECH

Online simulations can provide a faster, cleaner, easier way for students to make sense out of the information. However, what if that's not the goal? What if there's a cost in going for faster, cleaner, and easier? There's something powerful about the tangible element in a low-tech simulation because it forces students to use their imagination. This tactile element is something we sometimes lose sight on as we push toward all things digital. Yes, online games are great. True, virtual reality is just beginning to take off. However, physical simulations remind us that we can make our own world virtual through the power of imagination.

Furthermore, physical simulations are typically less programmed. They're more adaptable, which means you can modify them for your context. Also, they don't require an additional interface in order to use them. Our screens can create an artificial distance that we don't want in a simulation. When my students created a Chinese trade simulation, we could see the changes in prices firsthand. If we had participated in an on-screen simulation, it would have felt distant.

Note that simulations work best when dealing with abstract ideas and complex systems. It's critical that we avoid creating games that might trivialize injustice or human destruction (a slavery simulation, for example). Instead, focus on using games for conceptual development. A predator and prey version of tag can help students think about the food chain, but a simulation showing how stanzas work will probably fail as a lesson. Although some of the best games focus on human systems, you can create immersive systems that aren't quite as humanistic. I once saw a game called Integer Wars that helped students determine what to do with positive and negative integers. It was simple but it had the best elements of game-play, including a challenge, suspense, and incremental success.

OTHER WAYS TO INSPIRE IMAGINATION

While game-based learning and play can help students remain imaginative, we can't always integrate those into our units. However, here are a few strategies we can use.

#1
INTEGRATE THE ARTS

The arts inspire imagination. Remember the NASA engineer who was inspired to do origami after reading a book and seeing examples? There are countless other examples of students who were able to imagine new possibilities because of art, music, and literature. This is also why we need to carve out time for choice-based silent reading. As I mentioned earlier in this chapter, when students read, they visually design the world that the author describes using only words. The same imaginative process can happen with audiobooks as well. However, students also engage in imaginative thinking when they make sense out of informational texts and imagine concepts visual.

#2
UTILIZE VISUAL THINKING STRATEGIES

When students sketch-note their thoughts, they imagine the information and bridge a gap between the abstract and the concrete. Similarly, when they use visual thinking strategies[100] such on chart paper and sticky notes, they have to imagine the information in a visual format.

#3
ENCOURAGE HANDS-ON MAKER PROJECTS

When I interview entrepreneurs and innovators, I love to ask them about their childhood experiences. One of the most common activities I hear about is Legos. They describe following the meticulous directions and then later deviating from the plans and inventing something entirely new. Legos are inherently lo-fi and impractical. However, they tap into a child's natural imagination. While we can't always use Legos in school, we can incorporate elements of hands-on maker projects to inspire imagination. Similarly, students have the opportunity to imagine new creations when we incorporate divergent thinking activities into our weekly plans.

#4
ENCOURAGE "WHAT IF" QUESTIONS

Help students explore the "what if" questions to imagine new possibilities. In a history class, they might ask, "What would have happened if this event had ended differently?" In a science class, they might ask, "What if we changed the weight and the size of objects that we drop? What would happen?" These what-if questions push students out of the present and into the world of possibilities. Over time, this becomes a habit of the mind that inspires them to become innovators and makers.

#5
EMBRACE THE IMPRACTICAL

Schools tend to focus on the practicality of information. However, imagination is often impractical. It's a willingness to dream up things that might not work at first. And out of the impractical, the imagination grows and suddenly you're finding unique practical ideas that nobody else sees. This is why we need creative writing, even if students might never become fiction authors or poets or novelists. I love using impractical and quirky writing prompts that force students to be imaginative. Here are a few examples:

- Create a to do list for a villain.
- Write a diary from the perspective of your pet.
- Tell the story of Superman's underachieving brother, Carl.
- You just became a real estate agent for magical homes.

These prompts are not practical. They will not prepare students for a specific job in the future. They are, for lack of a better term, silly. And, as odd as it may seem, when they get excited about these prompts, they engage in creative, imaginative writing. This not only helps them remain imaginative. It also increases their writing fluency and motivation.

#6
REDUCE THE FEAR OF IMPERFECTION

This is a challenging one. In my experience, students become less imaginative when they work toward a higher grade. In the process, they grow risk-averse because they are scared that they'll lose points if they make a mistake. As educators, we need to find ways to reduce fear and promote intellectual risk-taking.

#7
PILOT DESIGN THINKING

While impractical, fantastical imagination is important, students can also engage in a much more practical type of imagination. With design thinking, they begin with awareness and move into inquiry. Here, they are engaging in those "what if questions" I just mentioned. Next, they engage in research, where they use their imagination to visualize and conceptualize information. This leads to ideation, where they are imagining an entirely new concept. Then they create and revise, where they have the opportunity to see the hands-on manifestation of imagination. As they move through iterations, they grow less risk-averse and more imaginative. Note that we'll be getting into design thinking and project-based learning in the next chapter.

HOW IMAGINATION CAN CHANGE A CLASS CULTURE

Chrissy Romano had a challenging group of students. Although she was a master teacher, she found it challenging to build a culture of respect. One critical moment occurred when she introduced a BreakoutEDU challenge. She first reviewed expectations around communication and collaboration. Then, she let them work on a breakout box (similar to an escape room).

"It can be very stressful. It can get frustrating for students." However, she noticed a change. Despite the frustration, they were engaged. Because it had a low barrier of entry, nearly every student participated. Some of the students who struggled the most academically thrived with this challenge.

This activity helped students to empathize with one another and work collaboratively. They saw the tangible benefit of working interdependently. "It was a turning point. It clicked for us."

By the end of the year, students were working collaboratively on a regular basis. They launched a Kids Camp unconference (based on open conversations and big ideas) and built a partnership with the kindergarten class. They took on bigger projects and excelled. This was, no doubt, the influence of Chrissy in developing a positive classroom culture. But one element of it was her strategic use of curiosity and imagination.

TRY THIS:
SIMULATIONS

If you're interested in sparking imagination, check out the creative writing and creative thinking prompts in the Vintage Innovation Toolkit, along with the less-than-practical writing prompts mentioned in this chapter. You can find these resources at vintageinnovationbook.com/toolkit.

CHAPTER 12

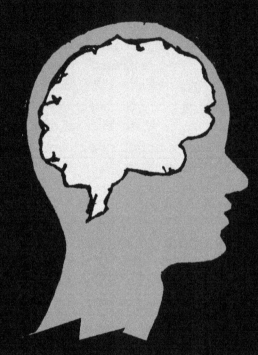

IN A DISTRACTED WORLD, OUR STUDENTS NEED TO ENGAGE IN

DEEP WORK

Neil Gaiman has the ability to take a reader out of their context and into a deeply imaginative world. I still remember sitting on an airplane, wiping away tears with a tiny cocktail napkin while reading *The Ocean at the End of the Lane*. I remember, too, the terror my daughter and I shared as we read *Coraline* on a rainy day. Although Gaiman makes it look effortless, this type of world-building and storycraft requires hours of intense, focused work.

Gaiman's secret weapon?

Boredom.

As he describes it, "I think it's about where ideas come from, they come from day dreaming, from drifting, that moment when you're just sitting there... The trouble with these days is that it's really hard to get bored. I have 2.4 million people on Twitter who will entertain me at any moment... it's really hard to get bored. I'm much better at putting my phone away, going for boring walks, actually trying to find the space to get bored in. That's what I've started saying to people who say 'I want to be a writer," I say 'great, get bored.'"[101]

Gaiman views boredom, not as something you allow, but as something you seek out. It is a gift and a discipline and a talent. Here, he deliberately rejects social media, email, and every other distraction that prevents him focused work.

While this might seem like the quirky habit of a fantasy writer, some of the most elite scientists, inventors, and engineers have used a similar approach to deep work. Charles Darwin used to schedule uninterrupted work time followed by a long walk, where he would let his mind wander as he tried to solve problems. Kahneman and Tversky, the founders of behavioral economics who shaped what we know about decision-making and motivation, would spend full days debating ideas and planning experiments in a space free of distractions.[102]

Cal Newport describes this as "deep work."[103] It's what happens when you are fully present for extended time on a single task or project. When you engage in deep work, you are more likely to hit a state of flow, where people hit a place where they are "in the zone." You feel fully alive, fully connected, and fully focused. Time seems to fly by. [104]

This sense of deep work is challenging in a world of incessant distractions. However, if we want students to become deep thinkers, they need to engage in deep work where they can develop the mental endurance to stick with a task long-term.

As educators, we can shift from action-packed lessons to larger learning segments that push students to think deeply and engage in deep work. But this requires a shift in our teaching from chopped-up, jam-packed lessons and into longer, uninterrupted period of project-based learning.

 # SLOWING DOWN

When I first began teaching, I ran a fast-paced classroom. In a 55-minute class period, I would aim for 5-6 transitions, with activities lasting no more than ten minutes. After all, "kids these days" had lower attention spans and needed a fast pace with more variety if I ever expected them to stay focused.

But then I noticed something. Kids could spend hours playing the same video game, lost in an immersive world. They could sit down and practice the chord progression to "Stairway to Heaven" (a rite of passage for any generation of kids learning the guitar) and they would spend two hours at a skate park attempting a kick-flip. Maybe "kids these days" aren't any different from kids in the past.

But I also realized that most of these activities - from silent reading to skateboarding to video games – began with student choice. They were able to push through the boredom, frustration, and fatigue because they cared about the task and they owned the process.

At the same time, I noticed that there were many students who seemed incapable of engaging in deep work. These students got bored easily and were quick to give up when a task was too challenging. When we did silent reading, they lasted five minutes at the most.

Eventually, I decided to change things up. Instead of having a class packed with quick transitions, I would slow things down with fewer stop-and-go moments and minimal distractions.

It didn't work at first. Students were actually more off-task in the beginning as they adjusted to the slower approach. But over time, I learned that deep work was a skill that my students could develop. As the year progressed, I noticed the transformation. The same students who had given up after five minutes of reading were begging me to let them continue with their novel toward the end of the school year.

Often, these students would zone in on a blog post they were writing or a sketch-note they were creating. They would wrestle with a math problem and if I offered help, they would say, "No, I got this." Or maybe they'd be working on a STEM challenge and the bell would ring and they didn't even notice it.

When students are able to reach this state of hyper-focus, they experience something researchers called "flow." [105]

Hungarian researcher Mihaly Csikszentmihalyi, puts it this way in *Flow: The Psychology of Optimal Experience*, [106] "The flow experience is when a person is completely involved in what he or she is doing, when the concentration is very high, when the person knows moment by moment what the next steps should be, like if you are playing tennis, you know where you want the ball to go, if you are playing a musical instrument you know what notes you want to play, every millisecond, almost. And you get feedback to what you're doing."

Flow requires the challenge to meet the skill level. It also requires frequent feedback, intrinsic motivation, and an extended period of time. These ideas are at the core of project-based learning, where students engage in meaningful projects with voice, choice, inquiry, and research.[107] [108] Students in my PBL-oriented class looked relaxed and even slower in the moment. However, they were actually more productive, more engaged, and thinking more deeply about the subject than in the traditional, fast-paced classroom. Looking back, my stop-and-go approach was a bit like a cruise through the city in rush hour. We were moving and stopping, winding around the busy streets, but not actually getting anywhere. By contrast, the PBL approach was more like a long, winding road through the country.

DEEP WORK THROUGH PROJECTS

Schools move at a frantic pace, with the bells and the announcements and the interruptions that occur on a regular basis. I can sometimes forget what it's like to have to scarf down a meal and run an errand in a twenty-two-minute lunch period. Most teachers I know have crowded curriculum maps punctuated by fire drills, assemblies, field trips, and testing days.

It can feel like you're simply adding another item onto an already crowded plate. However, PBL isn't about adding things to your plate. It's about re-arranging your plate so that students can work at a deeper level. But how does this actually work?

The following are specific strategies you can use to maximize time for PBL. Before getting into this, I want to share a quick caveat: it's all about context. There are so many human dynamics at work and ultimately, you know your students the best. You are the expert. Often, we learn through trial and error.

PBL ISN'T ABOUT ADDING
SOMETHING TO YOUR PLATE.

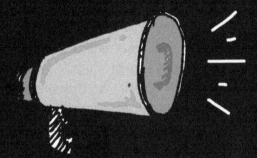

IT'S ABOUT REARRANGING
YOUR PLATE WITH A FOCUS
ON VOICE AND CHOICE.

#1
LESS TEACHER TALK

This was the hardest one for me as a middle school teacher. Direct instruction can feel so efficient as a way to convey information. And it is. You talk, they listen and take notes, and that's it. However, with PBL, students spend more time doing the work themselves. They ask more questions and find more of the answers on their own.

While this can feel less efficient, students often learn at a deeper level and retain the information for a longer period of time when they wrestle with it. It might not look as efficient but we actually save time by having students maximize their work time within a class period.

Often, the time-wasters are subtle. I remember asking a student teacher to do a time audit of how I spent my class time in a PBL unit. To my surprise, I spent way too much time giving directions and clarifying directions for the whole class. So, I tried something. I would write the directions on the board and then answer clarifying questions as I walked around the room. It worked.

#2
SHORTEN THE TIMELINE (BUT BUILD IN WIGGLE ROOM)

Ever noticed that students tend to waste time at the beginning or middle of a project and then rush toward the end to get it done? It turns out, we tend to work harder on a task when we are close to finishing it. By contrast, there's an idea called Parkinson's Law, that explains how "work expands to the time allotted."[109] In other words, if you give yourself three weeks to do a project and it should only take two weeks, you will find a way to use all three weeks rather than finish early.

Now, there are definitely times when students rush through projects and finish early. However, often students will spend longer than normal on a project because the timelines are too loose. I've found that it's easier to set tighter deadlines and then give students some additional days rather than creating really loose time deadlines. It helps to break projects into phases, which is why I love design thinking. With the LAUNCH Cycle, A.J. Juliani and created have specific phases that students walk through as they engage in creative work. You can check out the diagram on the next page.[110]

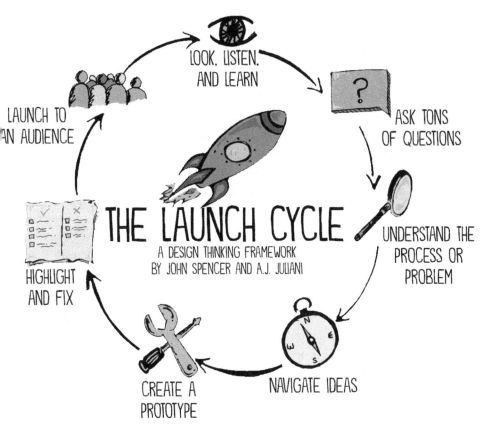

With the LAUNCH Cycle, students move through inquiry, research, ideation, prototyping, and revision in distinct phases. It also helps to have students keep track of their own progress by teaching them to engage in project management.

It helps to think of the LAUNCH Cycle as a framework for creativity and PBL as an instructional framework. It's similar to a science teacher who does an inquiry-based unit (instructional framework) but students use the scientific method as their science framework.

Even with these structures, sometimes students struggle to meet deadlines, which leads to my next point.

#3
FOCUS ON QUALITY OVER QUANTITY

When I first began teaching, I would wait for the slowest student to finish an assignment before moving on as a class. So, when it took a student thirty-five minutes to write a paragraph, we would all wait thirty-five minutes. I then stuck with that same timeframe for the entire year. A few months into the school year, I had students fill out a survey on my teaching and, to my surprise, the biggest complaint was that we were moving too slowly.

This was a breakthrough for me. What if I got rid of the requirements around quantity and instead focused on quality? So, during a warm-up, I said, "Try and write at least a paragraph. Many of you will do two or three but the goal should be to get your thoughts across clearly." They had high expectations but looser instructions.

When I switched to loosely structured assignments, students began to thrive. I no longer had students getting bored and off-task because they had finished early but I also didn't have the students who were scared of being behind all the time.

When we worked on blogging projects, I had students who wrote ten blog posts and others who wrote three. I had students who wrote 2,000-word posts and others who wrote three hundred words. Initially, there were questions of equity and fairness but because we framed it through the lens of personal goals, students realized that equity isn't about sameness. It's about helping each student reach their full potential. When we discussed it as a class, I would compare it to silent reading time, when each student read a different number of pages. Although it feels counterintuitive, this flexible approach actually saves time, because each student is more likely to work toward their maximum potential.

#4
USE STRUCTURES TO SAVE TIME

Early on in my PBL journey, I told students, "I want you to create a documentary. You need to develop a plan and then make it happen." It didn't happen. Students stood around talking without getting started. The larger project was too daunting, so I began to incorporate structures that would build interdependence and collaboration.

Structures are actually vital for creative productivity. It turns out people who are inexperienced at a task often fail to plan and have more false starts and mistakes while those who are experts tend to plan ahead.[111] Structures provide the necessary creative constraint to push divergent thinking and they help facilitate the actual work of creative work. Nearly every discipline uses a framework or blueprint for their creative work, it's a writer's workshop structure, an engineering process, the scientific method, or a design thinking framework. When we incorporate these frameworks into our PBL units, we not only save time, but we also teach students how to do creative work in various disciplines.

ACTUALLY, STRUCTURE CAN INSPIRE AND SUPPORT CREATIVITY

#5
GROUP YOUR STANDARDS

When I was a kid, we often learned skills in isolation and moved systematically from skill to skill. However, with PBL, students work on multiple, interconnected standards at the same time instead of going sequentially through each standard. When this happens, students move more slowly through the standards rather than going through the stop-and-go traditional methods. Often, they practice skills while also learning concepts.

In some cases, you might go fully competency-based and allow students to skip standards that they have already mastered.[112] For example, in the research phase of a project, students can work on specific reading skills they need to master and skip the skills they have already mastered. One student might be drawing conclusions while another is making inferences. In a design project, students might do statistical analysis connecting to the math standards and as the teacher, you can pull small groups to reinforce key skills and concepts.

Although I love longer PBL units, there are times when it helps to use a choice menu for a mini-project. Here's an example of a choice menu where students can choose the learning targets, resources, and end product.

As a teacher, I keep a list of learning targets and copy and paste those into the left column. I also keep an ongoing online curation of resources for each unit that I teach which I place in the middle column. Any time I see something fascinating or relevant, I copy and paste the link into a document. Then, I use that curated list of resources in the choice menus. When students chose podcasts, videos, etc., I link the option to a one-page document with tutorials, instructions, and rubrics for that particular option.

Learning Targets	Resources	Product
(Choose 1-2 that you currently haven't mastered)	Choose at least 3 resources that you will use to learn about the content.	Choose how you will demonstrate your mastery of the content.
Here's where you list optional learning targets. Example in math: I can identify a linear function by examining a graph. Example in social studies: I can determine the impact of World War II on the women's rights movement	Here's where you link curated resources, such as videos, podcasts, articles, infographics, and models. Example in math: Crash Course Videos Tutorial Article Flip Video from a classmate Examples: History podcast Article from Atlas Obscura Primary source documents	Here's where you list options for what students will create to demonstrate their learning. This might be a blog post, essay, slideshow, podcast, model, etc. Example in math: Video explaining how you solved it Example in social studies Podcast explaining women's involvement in World War II war effort

If students were learning about forces and motion in science, they might select a specific learning target. Then they would watch a video or podcast and then click on the slideshow option where they could see reminders of best practices (remember to use visuals, use a solid contrast in colors, cite sources, etc.) and begin creating their product.

Notice that with this choice menu, students are deciding either the topics, concepts, or skills and then deciding on their own resources and strategies before ultimately deciding on their final product. This typically takes 1-3 class periods, depending on the complexity of the learning targets and the end products. I found that this worked well in the following contexts:

- Early on in a unit, when they need to increase background knowledge
- Toward the end of the unit, when they need to own the intervention process
- When completing standards that don't work as well with project-based learning or design thinking
- In the moments when there is a time crunch and they don't have as much time to search for resources or where some of the online resources actually reinforce misconceptions

- If you are just making the leap into student-driven learning and you want to start with something that builds on student choice but doesn't require a massive project

Notice how students are able to engage in deep work because they are working at their own pace. By self-selecting the learning targets, they are able to focus on standards that they still need to master. As they move through the curated resources and eventually to the demonstration of their learning through a product, they are not tied to rigid time deadlines. As a result, students learn how to engage in focused, self-directed deep work.

#6
TEACH NEW CONTENT THROUGH THE PROJECT

One of the key differences between a culminating project and a PBL unit is that students should be learning *through* a project rather than learning first and then doing completing the project afterward.

Note that you will still need to do direct instruction and you might even begin your project with a quick concept attainment lesson. John Hattie recommends focusing on concept attainment before ever moving into student inquiry.[113] Moreover, there are times when you might need to review a concept or a skill together with students before they move into a new phase of their projects. However, these more traditional approaches should occur throughout the project. The goal is to integrate direct instruction in a way that feels authentic.

#7
ASSESS AS YOU GO

With project-based learning, you can incorporate frequent formative assessments into each phase of the project. Here you treat assessment more like a verb than a noun. It's something you do rather than something you take. You can also embed self-assessments, peer feedback, and shorter five-minute student-teacher conferences so that they can set goals and clarify their mastery of the content. In the process, you save time, because you are not having students completing tests or weekly quizzes. Admittedly, this can feel risky. However, the longer you engage in an "assess as you go" approach, the more natural it begins to feel.

SHOULD WE BAN THE DEVICES?

We ran into some major road bumps when I first shifted toward a more "deep work" approach. Although we had a few class discussions and the occasional direct instruction, our mix of project-based learning and design thinking meant that students spent the entire class period focused on one larger task and one major project. Many students lacked creative endurance. They struggled to hit a state of flow in their work, so they spent the first week going to YouTube or checking their Instagram feed.

It's easy to blame the devices. Just take the computers away and you'll be fine. However, I wonder if that's a little shortsighted. What if instead of outright banning devices, we helped students figure out how to create their own self-imposed bans? What if we helped students determine how to engage in deep work while also having smart phones?

In my experience, most students can learn how to self-manage with their devices. Often, the same students who were distracted during the first few weeks would begin developing more endurance a few weeks later. Suddenly, they were editing videos, writing blog posts, and crafting code. In other words, they were engaged in deep work. It's easy to ban devices. It's harder to focus on how to use our devices wisely.

Ultimately, students learned how to engage in deep work when they were fully engaged in meaningful projects. I learned that the issue wasn't the devices. It was the culture of distractions and amusement that dominated the way they had been using devices. As they learned to engage in meaningful projects, they developed the endurance to engage in deep work.

For what it's worth, students have been distracted for decades, if not centuries. When I was in school, we played this horrible violent game where you would get hung if you couldn't spell things correctly. It was called Hang Man. We sent texts via notes from torn paper. We used Cootie Catchers to predict the future. Our minds wandered during teacher lectures. True, technology has accelerated the number of distractions. But the answer is the same one that has existed for years – deeper, more meaningful work. Ultimately, this deep work thrives when we embrace project-based learning.

TRY THIS: MINI PROJECTS

Vintage Innovation Resources

One way to pilot PBL is through a mini-project. You can try out a Choice-Based Mini-Project in the Vintage Innovation Toolkit at vintageinnovationbook.com/toolkit. I have also included a longer design thinking project if you want to test out the LAUNCH Cycle.

CHAPTER 13

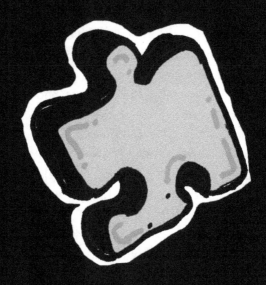

IN A WORLD OF ENDLESS POSSIBILITIES, OUR STUDENTS NEED TO BE

CURIOUS

When I was a kid, if I had a question, we had to drive to the library, sift through the card catalogue, and navigate the dark art of microfiche. Now, we can hop onto the computer and find answer in seconds. Figuratively, of course. Most computers can't handle the weight of being hopped on by a grown man.

This increase in knowledge should boost curiosity. After all, most experts tend to be infinitely curious about their areas of expertise. I've never heard of a cosmologist who says, "I'm done with the universe. No more questions here." I've also never seen an engineer who says, "I'm an expert now. I really don't need to figure out how stuff works." Nor have I seen any historians who say, "I don't really care what happened in the past." Novelists tend to have stacks of books that they want to read. Even the most seasoned chefs are always out searching for new cuisine (see what I did there).

And yet, we don't always see this curiosity in our students. We've all seen high-achievers who play the game of school. They figure out what's on the test only to forget it the next week. You see it, too, in the low-achievers, who have defined themselves as "not any good" at a subject and have given up asking questions. You see it in the young artists who learned to color inside the lines and the young scientists who learned their question was "off-topic."

In school, there's often a focus on staying on-task and covering the curriculum map. Despite the flaws in the system, there are so many teachers out there who are sparking curiosity in their students every single day. These teachers are designing learning experiences that get kids asking "why?" and "how?" You can see it in their classrooms. There's an energy and excitement about discovering new ideas. And this curiosity is exactly what students will need for the future. If we go back to Tetlock's research on the "super forecasters," they were the ones who were open-minded and curious.

"IF STUDENTS LEAVE
SCHOOL LESS CURIOUS
THAN WHEN
THEY STARTED,
WE HAVE FAILED THEM."

– GEORGE COUROS –

There are science teachers asking students to design their own science experiments and language arts teachers asking students to do question-generated research as they craft blog posts and articles. There are social studies teachers inspiring students to ask questions about the past and mathematics teachers encouraging students to get curious about solving problems and finding new approaches. While these moments seem small, they are the building blocks for lifelong curiosity.

Students should leave our schools wondering and questioning and seeking out multiple answers and new perspectives. But to do that we might actually need to make school more confusing.

 # THE MYSTERY SHIP

Picture this. The year is 1978 and you are part of a construction crew in downtown San Francisco. It's a time of disco and progressive rock and an underground punk scene. But you're about to find something underground that you never expected to see – a ship buried 20 feet underground. It's not just any ship. It's a ship from the 1800's and it's miles inland from the ocean.

However, this ship was not part of a shipwreck. It's still mostly intact and it's filled with bricks, nails, tin plates, boots, shovels, jackets, and bottles that seem to be well over a hundred years old. Moreover, this ship is the middle of downtown instead of being right off the coast.

So, what happened? How did this ship end up so far away from the ocean? Why did this ship remain buried for years without being discovered? What purpose did this ship once serve? Who owned it? When did it become buried? What do you think of the items that were used? What clues do they offer about the age of the ship?

You must create a theory about what the ship was and why it's buried in the middle of downtown San Francisco.

This was the prompt I created for my students. I placed them into teams of four and had them debate potential scenarios. I then allowed them to ask me yes or no questions. I asked them to put their devices away and debate their theories. Slowly, I added additional clues and asked them to refine their theory.

When they couldn't solve it, I said, I said, "I'm now going to share the correct answer" and they begged me to give them another five minutes.

This was the opposite of a typical history lesson. Instead of making it simpler with charts and diagrams, I added complexity with multiple clues. Instead of going for clarity, I deliberately confused them. However, the mystery pushed their thinking and increased their engagement with the content.

Don't get me wrong. The answer to the boat mystery is fascinating. It has to do with filling in swampy land and essentially building land in an area where land didn't already exist. But the answer becomes so much more interesting after a period of wading in confusion. The confusion is what leads to wonder and ultimately engagement.

SHOULD SCHOOL BE MORE CONFUSING?

I was recently at a technology conference where the speaker said, "If a student can Google it, we shouldn't be teaching it."

I see his point. However, it had me thinking about the mystery ship lesson. I had actually required my students to put their devices away. They could have Googled it and found the answer in seconds. Actually, they could have asked Alexa or Siri or Cortana. Just kidding. Nobody talks to Cortana. I bet she feels lonely sometimes.

But still . . . there was something in the mystery that pushed my students to think deeper. They were more curious each time they had a new theory debunked. The confusion led to deeper thinking and better learning.

As I wrote this book, I spent three months focused on reading works that were at least 2,000 years old or older. I wanted to uncover old ideas that we should reconsider in our current context. I wanted to listen to voices that have been hushed by distance and context. While their philosophies differed, I noticed a common trend. Most of these works were confusing. It wasn't an issue of text complexity, archaic language, or cultural knowledge of ancient civilizations. Rather, these texts were deliberately confusing.

The ancient texts reminded me to embrace paradox and mystery. They made no attempt to get the point across quickly. Instead, they forced me to slow down and embrace the mystery. Whether I was reading a parable, a story, or a Socratic dialogue, I realized that confusion was a vital part of learning.

Confusion pushes you to slow down and think deeper. This struggle to figure things out means the information actually sticks. It's why I forget entire sections of textbooks but it's really hard to forget a confusing parable. It often leads you into a place of nuanced understanding.

Annie Murphy Paul describes it this way: "We short-circuit this process of subconscious learning, however, when we rush in too soon with an answer. It's better to allow that confused, confounded feeling to last a little longer—for two reasons. First, not knowing the single correct way to resolve a problem allows us to explore a wide variety of potential explanations, thereby giving us a deeper and broader sense of the issues involved. Second, the feeling of being confused, of not knowing what's up, creates a powerful drive to figure it out. We're motivated to look more deeply, search more vigorously for a solution, and in so doing we see and understand things we would not have, had we simply been handed the answer at the outset."[114]

However, schools aren't built around confusion. Our standardized tests place a high value in speed and accuracy rather than nuance and confusion. We value teachers who can make learning efficient, clear, and easy-to-understand. In teacher preparation programs, we learn to create concise lessons that waste little time.

But I wonder if we're missing something in this push toward efficiency and simplicity. Derek Muller has published some fascinating research on science videos.[115] When people watch simple videos with clear concepts, they tend to believe that they understand it at a deep level, but that's not the case. They are overconfident in their understanding and unaware of what they don't know. They're also less engaged mentally as they watch it.

By contrast, when they watch videos with strategic confusion (especially those that push them to make and test a hypothesis) they are convinced that they know very little of the information when, in fact, they are learning it at a deeper level. They also have higher engagement and deeper retention.

I find this fascinating because we often assume that students are failing to understand concepts because we are making them too confusing. So, we go for simpler texts and more easily digestible content. But what if this is wrong? What if deeper, more authentic, engagement looks less like a Khan Academy video and more like a Socratic Dialogue?

USING STRATEGIC CONFUSION

The following are specific strategies teachers can use to integrate strategic confusion into the learning experience.

Present mysteries. Provide students with scenarios that are deliberately and strategically confusing and then let them posit their own hypotheses.

Allow for mistakes. Let them see that being "wrong" is actually what scientists, historians, engineers, and mathematicians do on a regular basis.

Embrace student inquiry. Whether it's a philosophical discussion or a hands-on science experiment, allow students to ask tons of questions.

Don't shy away from confusing material. In other words, read works that are confusing. Watch movies that perplex you. Read up on the Early Socratic Dialogues even when they don't seem to resolve themselves easily.

Avoid simplistic explanations. Kids learn that plants turn our breath into food. Not true. The answer is much more complicated and fascinating. These simplistic answers actually reinforce misconceptions and fail to recognize that younger students can actually handle nuance.

Encourage dialogue. As I go back to the ancient sources, I'm struck by the power in confusing dialogue. It's inefficient. It's messy. But it pushes you into areas of thinking that you'll miss when reading a simple chart. The same is true in a classroom.

Students need to have the space and time to debate ideas and engage in deep dialogue.

Test your answers. This takes some self-discipline, but it's the idea of intentionally holding back on a definitive answer. It's what happens when you have a general idea but then you decide to go back and test it instead of declaring it as the absolute answer.

Identify what you don't know. Students will learn things at a deeper level when you make a prediction and then figure out just how wrong you actually are. This sense of confusion then fuels your engagement, inquiry, and learning.

When we use confusion strategically, students will be frustrated. Some of them will get angry. But they will also be engaged. They will slow down and think deeper about the content. The end result is a humbler and more nuanced understanding of the content.

While strategic confusion is a teacher-centered approach to ignite curiosity, you can also take a different approach where you encourage students to pursue their own questions and find their own answers.

PILOT INQUIRY-BASED LEARNING

Often, students internalize the message that uncertainty is a sign of failure. But with inquiry-based learning, students are able to tap into that curiosity, engage in research, and ultimately create a product for an authentic audience. In the process, you begin to transform the classroom into a culture of curiosity. They view uncertainty as the start of authentic learning.

Let's take a real-world example. Just kidding. Let's look at a fantastical example. In *The Order of Phoenix*, the fifth of the Harry Potter series, Dolorus Umbridge takes over as the Defense Against the Dark Arts teacher and instantly transforms the class into a text-book-based class focused on passing the standardized tests. When Harry questions whether this will prepare them for the chaos of fighting against Vold . . . err . . . um . . . he who must not be named . . . Umbridge punishes him and he ends up forming his own school within a school called Dumbledore's Army.

Dumbledore's Army is purely inquiry-based. While Harry is the teacher, he is mostly a guide on the side, empowering the students to ask questions and find the answers themselves. They rely on each other and on various spell books to solve problems and answer their questions. While the process might seem messy compared to Umbridge's approach, the students learn at a rapid pace because they aren't wasting time repeating what they already know. This is an example of inquiry-based learning.

WHAT DO WE MEAN BY STUDENT INQUIRY?

The inquiry-centered approach has existed for thousands of years. Socrates and Confucius both used variations on this format. It's a critical component of the scientific method of the early enlightenment and it was a core idea within both Dewey and Montessori's notions of student-centered learning.

Margus Pedaste shares a model of the four phases of inquiry. It starts with orientation, which is often a discussion.[116] From there, it moves into conceptualization, where students generate questions and define a hypothesis. This leads to investigation, where students explore, experiment, and interpret data, often in a way that is flexible and dynamic. Finally, they move to a conclusion. Note that this model of inquiry still includes direct instruction. Even within inquiry-based learning, teachers still need to include a period of skill development and concept attainment.

Sometimes students need a gradual release approach to inquiry. Heather Banchi and Randy Bell define four different types of inquiry that you can view on a spectrum from teacher-centered / structured to learner-centered / open.[117]

- Level 1 is **Confirmation Inquiry**, where the teacher teaches the concepts, creates the questions, and models the process for students.
- Level 2 is **Structured Inquiry**, where the teacher creates the initial questions and shares the procedures then students walk through the rest of the inquiry process by collecting data, analyzing data, and drawing conclusions.
- Level 3 is **Guided Inquiry**, where the teacher provides the research questions but students own the research or experimentation process.
- Level 4 is **Open/True Inquiry**. Here students formulate their own questions, design their own experiments or research, collect their own data, and share their findings.

According to Banchi and Bell, teachers should start with levels 1 and 2 and use those as scaffolding, so that students can learn the inquiry process. However, in my experience, there is power in asking students to engage in Level 4 inquiry, where they are truly empowered to ask their own questions and engage in their own research.

WHAT ABOUT THE STANDARDS?

This sounds great but many of us have specific standards we need to teach. How do we pull off inquiry-based learning with a curriculum map?

The easiest approach is to find the topic-neutral standards. Often, these are process or skills standards. For example, in Language Arts it might be the informational reading and writing standards that connect to the research process. In social studies, it might be the standards that address broad themes rather than specific historical events. In science, students might learn about the Scientific Method.

Sometimes, though, you can find the wiggle room within concept-based standards. For example, students might need to learn about specific topics in a forces and motion unit in science. However, they can ask questions and explore their curiosity within this broader topic.

WHAT DOES THIS LOOK LIKE?

Inquiry-based learning can be something as large as a year-long Genius Hour project or as small as a 60-minute Wonder Day Project. Because the subject tends to be topic-neutral, you can allow them to pursue a more open form of inquiry. Here are a few examples of what it looks like in each subject:

Science: An inquiry-based lesson could be a short exploration of a phenomenon, where the teacher models a process and asks students to generate questions. It could be a single-day research question where they get to explore any science question they want. Or it might be a scientific experiment. For example, we used to do *Myth Buster* styled project where students would test out urban legends.

Math: Dan Meyer has a great approach to inquiry with his "What can you do with it?" problems. Here, teachers provide a scenario and students get the opportunity to ask their own questions and then compare strategies. Other times, students might ask a statistics-related question and then gather data and interpret results.[118]

History: As a teacher, you might provide an open-ended prompt of "what are you curious about?" or "what question would you want to explore if that were an option." We used to do history-related Genius Hour blogs, where students explored any history they found interesting. As a teacher, I learned the fascinating history of ice cream, hair, skateboarding, video games, and synthesizers. Here, students still had to master the social studies process standards while also creating timelines, listicles, informational posts, and editorials.

Health: I'm working with a pre-service teacher right now who is leading his health and P.E. classes through inquiry-based projects. In P.E., they are researching personal fitness and applying the research to their personal fitness goals. They're meeting one-on-one with their teacher, who provides expert guidance to make sure their information is safe. In health, his students are studying public health crises and researching the causes and effects before ultimately designing a PSA campaign. Their inquiry is ultimately leading to a series of products that could change the world.

Language Arts: Because reading and writing are content-neutral, students can work through short-term and long-term research with informational text. After asking their questions and finding sources, students get the chance to analyze their information and determine how they will share their findings. Students might create a Q&A blog post or a podcast explaining their research process. In this case, the final product is a chance to share their share their journey with an audience. Other times, this inquiry process leads to a larger product, where they synthesize their information into a documentary or a podcast series. When I taught middle school, my students would create CuriosityCasts, where they would pose a question and work through the research process of informational reading, followed by a recorded peer discussion.

If you teach younger students, you might have to provide additional scaffolding and curate specific resources for them. But there's a hidden advantage. Younger students are naturally curious. They're always asking questions. On the other hand, older students tend to have more background knowledge and can dive into more specific, obscure questions. It's an opportunity for them to have voice and choice and ownership.

MAKING INQUIRY A PRIORITY

When I first learned about inquiry-based learning, I scoffed at the idea. How do you pull it off with a complex set of standards? How do you do it with limited resources? I started with our Wonder Day Projects and eventually began finding more ways to tap into student curiosity.

But what about the high school level, where teachers have to worry about AP tests and heavy content?
I talked with Chris Lehmann, the principal at the Science Leadership Academy in Philadelphia, Pennsylvania. At SLA, teachers design inquiry-based projects and integrate both guided and open inquiry into everything they do. Lehmann describes it this

way, "It starts with inquiry. Teaching kids to ask powerful questions that are truly their own is how you develop voice and choice."

If you ever get a chance to visit the school, you'll notice that that curiosity is a part of the culture. Students are constantly asking questions. It goes beyond the subject matter. Students at SLA ask deep questions about the systems and structures of school itself.

As he describes it, ""critical question-askers become critical thinkers." But it's more than just critical thinking. The students at SLA are noticeably creative. They're more excited about what they're learning and they are learning it at a deeper level. But they also seem more confident than most high school students. There are so many factors at work: a school culture that honors student agency, teachers that incorporate student voice and choice, leadership that encourages experimentation and innovation. But right there in the mix is student curiosity.

But what about the tests and the standards? SLA is an urban public high school in the heart of Philadelphia. They have the same standards and expectations as other schools in the area. SLA students have to take the same tests, follow the same curriculum, and master the same standards as students in other public schools. "The key is to work with creative constraint so that you find the guided and open inquiry within the content you're required to teach."

This all begins with the teachers. According to Chris Lehmann, "The piece of the puzzle which is less obvious is when teachers engage in critical inquiry, they create a culture of inquiry. We should be asking those questions not just of the content but on all things. As teachers, we create the conditions that lead to deeper inquiry. But this also requires authentic listening. When we listen with intent and purpose, we create the space for voice and choice."

If we want students to own their learning, we need them to remain curious. And this is why inquiry-driven PBL is so powerful.

They grow into the curious, lifelong learners who end up changing the world. As Chris Lehmann describes it, "The goal is not to be the workers of the future but the citizens of the future; to be thoughtful, inquiry-driven humans."

TRY THIS:
WONDER DAY

If you'd like your students to embrace awe and wonder, consider piloting a Wonder Day Project. You can find the Wonder Day and Wonder Week Projects in the Vintage Innovation Toolkit at vintageinnovationbook.com/toolkit.

Vintage Innovation Resources

IT IS OFTEN THE CURIOUS ONE,
THE WANDERING WONDERER,
THE INCESSANT ASKER OF QUESTIONS,
WHO ULTIMATELY CHANGES THE WORLD

CHAPTER 14

IN A WORLD OF OF INSTANT INFORMATION, OUR STUDENTS NEED TO BE

CURATORS

We live in a world of instant information, where ideas go viral without much thought regarding accuracy and validity. It's a place where content is cheap. Cheap to make. Cheap to share. Cheap to consume. The traditional gatekeepers are gone, which is great for students. They can create and share their work in ways that were previously unimaginable.

But there's a cost. The best stuff doesn't always rise to the top. If we're not careful, we mistake the speed of consumption for the depth of knowledge. Our students will need to be critical consumers. To do that, they need to be curators.

WHAT IS CONTENT CURATION?

The best curators are the ultimate geeks. They develop their expertise by immersing themselves in a niche area while also making surprising connections between ideas in seemingly unrelated worlds. Curators find specific excerpts that are relevant at the moment but also timeless. They can explain the purpose, the context, and the necessity of what they are citing.

Although we tend to associate curators with museums, I'm drawn toward a more archaic definition of the term with an earthy connotation. Some linguists tie it back to the Medieval Latin word *curare*, which meant "to cure an illness." It had a connotation of providing loving attention and management. Other linguists tie the word "curator" goes back to the word *curatus*, which meant "spiritual guide" or "one responsible for the care of souls."[119]

Over time, this word morphed into a deep care and love for a particular subject, knowledge, or set of artistic works. Think of art curators who define the spaces of a museum. They know the works on a deep level and can explain the meaning and purpose in ways that make the work more relevant.[120]

CURATION IS ALL ABOUT
GEEKING OUT

Some of the best curators are able to tap into that original sense of being "one responsible for the care of souls." They care, not only about what the work means but about how it will make you a better person.

Although curators take their work seriously, there's also a touch of fun to it. Curators get really exciting about the content they consume.

TEACHERS ARE ALREADY CURATORS

We piece together resources, research, and ideas as we develop lessons. We curate the content that we teach. This isn't anything new or groundbreaking. It's what happens when we find a great book or video and share it with our students.

But what if we take this art of curation and teach it to our students as well? What if we empowered students to curate their own content? As teachers, we want our students to have both an excited passion and a nuanced care for what they are learning. We want them to pay attention to context and purpose in the information they consume. We want them to make connections and provide their own lens.

CURATION LEADS TO CREATIVITY

When we think of creativity, it's easy to picture a person coming up with something entirely new, pulling it from thin air and making it from scratch. But if you watch people engaged in creative work, they are often critical consumers of the same type of work they create. There's this ongoing cycle of critical consuming, inspiration, and creative work. As they create more, it leads to a deeper ability to consume critically, where they find more inspiration, and the cycle continues.

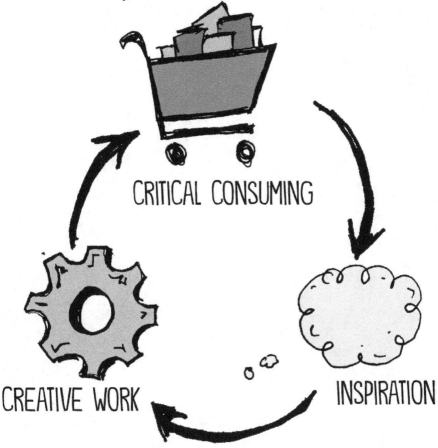

Chefs enjoy great meals. Musicians listen to great music. Engineers make sense out of what other people have designed. The better they are at consuming, the more likely they are to be inspired to create something new. In other words, critical consuming leads to inspiration, which leads to creative work. Here's where curation comes in. It helps students find the inspiration they will need for their creative work.[121]

CURATION IS THE BRIDGE BETWEEN CONSUMING AND CREATING

consuming   creating

In a previous chapter, I mentioned the failure of the futuristic Astrodome. However, Camden Yards worked because it began with curation. The architects began their design by searching through former designs of ballparks that had been demolished decades earlier. They began pulling together the asymmetrical design of Ebbets Field with the ivy in Forbes Field and the skyline view of Wrigley Field and Fenway Park.

If we go back to the consume to create cycle, the process of curation meant they were critical consumers of these older ideas that designers had ignored for decades. This led to deeper inspiration and ultimately creative ideas, which then spurred them toward more critical consuming, inspiration, and creative ideas.

But to be critical consumers, they needed to be curators. They had to filter out the ideas that were unimportant and hone in on the most necessary information. They needed to geek out on the styles of former ballparks in a way that was both celebratory and critical.

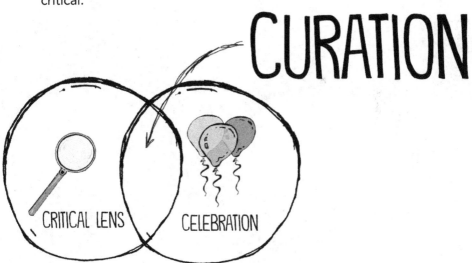

But what does curation actually look like?

THE CURATION PROCESS

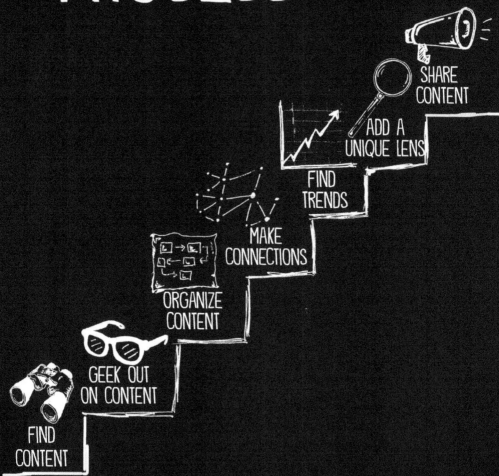

SHARE
CONTENT

ADD A
UNIQUE LENS

FIND
TRENDS

MAKE
CONNECTIONS

ORGANIZE
CONTENT

GEEK OUT
ON CONTENT

FIND
CONTENT

THE CURATION PROCESS

Content curation begins with an intense love of the content. Think of gallery curators. They get giddy over the seemingly random (and yet almost impossible to replicate) approach of Jackson Pollock. However, they can engage in a two-hour discussion on the relationship between kitsch art and postmodern philosophy. While there is an overlap with criticism, curators are more likely to geek out on the subject in a way that is explanatory instead of evaluative. This is often combined with a desire to make a work accessible to the public. Here are a few things that are a part of the curation process. Note that I share this as a sequential process but it is often much messier than this.

Searching for Content: The best curators are the ones who can find content that not everyone notices. This is what makes Maria Popova of Brain Pickings so amazing. She has this way of finding content that people are missing, looking in places we've overlooked.

Geeking Out on Content: The best curators are able to collect and consume great content. It's not mindless consumption. It is mindful and relaxed but also sharp and analytical. One of the things I've noticed about great curators is that they scribble notes all over the margins of their books and yet they feel the complete freedom to skim and skip when necessary. They know how to find the information that actually matters.

Organizing Content: Curation often involves placing content into categories or themes. Often, students will try and figure out the "right" way to organize the information, because schools typically teach students an external organizational system. However, this sense of classification is deeply personal and should mirror the way that students think. It's a chance to engage in tagging and categorizing in a way that feels meaningful to the students.

Making Connections: The best curators are able to find connections between seemingly opposite artists, ideas, or disciplines in ways that make you think, "Wow, I never considered that before."

Finding Trends: This aspect of curation is a little more analytical. Sometimes it even involves picking apart data or crunching numbers. It's the idea of looking at information across several spaces and finding specific trends. This is often where someone arrives at a different, counterintuitive conclusion.

Adding a Unique Lens: There's typically a certain clarity and brevity in the commentary curators add. When done well, a curator almost seems invisible, moving along the snippets of content. And yet, over time, you begin to appreciate the subtle personality and voice of a curator. If the critic and commentator can occasionally shout their opinions, the curator is gently whispering a relevant idea to a distracted culture.

Sharing the Content: Content curation has the end goal of getting great content into the hands of a larger audience. It is deliberately others-centered, even when the curator is introspective. Sometimes, the goal is to provide a set of practical information into the hands of readers. Others are more about offering something intriguing, even if it's not inherently practical.

Note that this isn't a new process. While the tools are now digital, people used this same curation process in the nineteenth century at the height of the commonplace book craze. It helps to imagine commonplace books as an old-school Pinterest at a time when people had muttonchops and suspenders and loved to pickle things and crochet; which, I suppose describes present-day Hipsters but also 19th Century Americans.

Back then, folks compiled commonplace books with scraps of recipes, letters, quotes, proverbs, political cartoons, and tables with weights and measures. They would add to these books over years, often passing them around from person to person. Often, they wrote comments in the margins and designed elaborate organizational systems to connect the ideas and resources.

Commonplace books emerged in an era when information was expensive and curation was cumbersome.[122] Technology changes. We can access information faster than ever. Our current problem isn't that information is expensive but that it's too cheap. But that's why we need digital commonplace books. Here students learn how to find, prioritize, organize, summarize, and communicate the important information they access on a regular basis.

GETTING STARTED WITH CONTENT CURATION

The following are a few tips for getting started with the content curation process.

Model content curation. Notice that few students walk into class with curation skills. We live in a consumer culture that values speed and amusement over slower, deliberate thought that is needed in curation. It's not surprising then, that teachers often need to model the curation process.

Let students geek out. Curators are natural geeks. They get excited about ideas and topics within their domain. They engage in research in a way that feels like an adventure. If we want students to engage in content curation, we need to let them geek out. Tap into their prior knowledge and let them run with it.

Spend more time on it. Content curation takes time. Take a look at any master curator and you'll see this commitment to time. There's no way around it. If you want to see students curate, you have to carve out specific time for it. However, we can integrate curation into the daily process of information consumption.

Begin earlier. Traditionally, teachers wait until the end of the year to have students do research. It's usually part of a multi-week project. If you begin at the beginning of the year, they will slowly learn the art of curation as the year progresses.

Let students own the process. They should choose the topics, the questions, and the sources they find interesting. This could connect to research, silent reading, blogging, or Genius Hour. It's also important to let students choose the platform. Curation can happen in a journal or a notebook if they want to keep it private. Or it could happen in a blog, in a podcast, or in a video series. In some cases, visual curation sites like Pinterest can work for students who want to organize things in a spatial manner.

WANT TO GET STARTED WITH CONTENT CURATION?

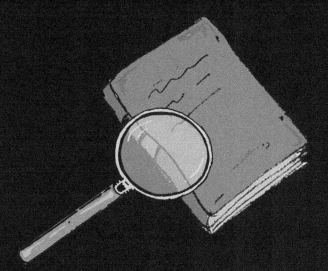

CONNECT WITH YOUR

LIBRARIAN

CONNECT WITH YOUR SCHOOL LIBRARIAN

"If we have the internet, why do we still need librarians?" This is something I've heard since the days of dial-up and continue to hear right now. It misses the vital role that librarians play in our students' lives. It's true that the information landscape has changed. It is easier than ever to create a work and publish it to the world and with a tap of a button, we access information from anywhere at any time.

But actually, that's why librarians are more vital than ever. In an age of instant information, librarians help students learn to ask better questions, find valid sources, and deconstruct the information. Take a quick glance at the false information shared on social media. Case in point, I've seen friends who are convinced that the world is flat. We are in desperate need of media literacy and librarians are the ones best poised to make this a reality.

Moreover, librarians teach students the art and science of content curation, where they learn to connect ideas from multiple sources and apply a unique lens to the information.

But content curation isn't simply a matter of gathering resources. It's about igniting a passion for reading and tapping into geeky interests. Librarians ignite a passion for learning, whether a student is gathering together informational texts or getting lost in a fantastical world of fiction. Librarians remind students that research should be fun.

Many of us work in a high-stakes testing system, where students often answer questions to get a grade and prepare for the test. People refer to the standardized test as the 800-pound elephant in the room. But it's more like a demigorgan from *Stranger Things*: invisible, powerful, and ready to pull people into the upside down. Librarians are the slayers of Demogorgans, reminding us to focus on what really matters: growing in wisdom. They are the ever-present curators, calling our students into an ancient art that's more vital than ever before.

In a world of constant noise and shallow distraction, librarians step in and inspire creativity, critical thinking, empathy, and systems thinking. In other words, they help our children become the kind of people we want them to be.

CURATION IN ALL SUBJECTS

We tend to think of curation as a part of the humanities. Students might curate fascinating information from World War I or curate styles of art in an art history class. Maybe they curate their favorite novels from a particular genre in reading or share their geeky interests via informational text in language arts.

However, curation can also work in math and science. I once had a student who had a biology-themed Pinterest board with curated pictures and facts of deep sea creatures and marsupials and strange birds. A decade later, she's now finishing her biology degree.

Students might gather together their favorite engineering designs for a STEM class or compile fascinating statistics in a math course.

This sounds great but what about younger students? Actually, younger students are natural curators. While the organizational system might be a little simpler, you'll easily find preschoolers gathering rocks and bugs they find on the playground. First graders argue about dinosaurs and squishy toys. They are constantly geeking out. In fact, elementary students live for one of the most vintage classroom activities around: show-and-tell.

When students become curators, they have new ideas and perspectives that will ultimately make them experts in multiple fields. They learn to combine ideas and find connections between unrelated sources.

FINDING YOUR HIDDEN GENIUS

When I first launched our Social Voice blog, I limited topics to what I considered "real" social studies topics. But then I had a group of students ask if they could write a fashion section. Initially, I scoffed at this idea. I thought fashion was shallow and trivial.

I was wrong.

This small group threw themselves into the curation process and ultimately used that to craft deep and profound blogs. Marissa wrote a blog post about the "politics of hair," by documenting what it was like to be African-American and have to decide whether to wear her hair natural or straighten it. Another student wrote a post about school uniforms. Still another crafted a heart-breaking reflection on gender expectations as an openly gay student, his love of fashion, and why he felt trapped in eighth grade. I learned that there is no such thing as a shallow topic; just a shallow way of thinking about topics.

I also made the mistake of focusing on the best writers. I would tell students, "if you don't want to write public posts, you don't have to." While my goal was to honor student agency, I did little to encourage struggling writers to share their work.

But a few years later, after we had switched from a class blog to individual blogs, I asked students to share at least one work with a larger audience. I had just co-designed Write About, which would allow my students to send their work to topic-based groups like "Animal Lovers" and "Car Fanatics."

One boy really struggled with writing. It took him a full week to do an outline and write a single blog post. Most students knew him as the quiet kid who never spoke. Even with the team-builder activities we had done, he still stuck to himself most of the time.

One afternoon, he finished his blog post and pressed "publish" instead of "save as a draft."

My heart sank as I noticed the post pop up into my class feed with words "7 comments" next to it. Middle schoolers can be brutal. I was so sure that they had picked on him for his sloppy grammar and bad punctuation.

But that's not what happened. Instead, the comments were affirming.

"I love that game, too," a boy wrote.

"I just got into it. What advice do you have?" another kid commented.

He had an audience. And though his writing remained shaky, he began sharing cheat codes he had discovered and patterns he had noticed that nobody else could see.

He had an audience. He had a voice. He was an author.

Most of those students will never become professional journalists. But they taught me so much about citizenship and journalism and what it means to choose kindness and empathy in our digital spaces.

TRY THIS:
CONTENT CURATION

Get started with content curation with a content curation protocol, a sketch video explanation, and a list of ideas for various subject areas. You can find all of these resources in the Vintage Innovation Toolkit at vintageinnovationbook.com/toolkit.

CHAPTER 15

USING A FOOD TRUCK APPROACH

When we think of innovative companies, it's easy to imagine an open-air tech startup with table tennis tables and free drinks and huge windows and chairs so modern you're not sure how you're supposed to sit in them or look at them. Sometimes I look at those spaces and think,

"Man, I wish schools were more like this." But they're not. Schools don't have millions in startup money flowing into making the spaces perfect. And, while these companies often look amazing, many of the startups go bankrupt within the first three years.

Meanwhile, some of the most innovative ideas are happening in much more humble environments —greasy, tiny kitchens parked by the side of busy streets. If you want to find innovation, look no further than your local food truck. Food trucks continue to redefine the way we view food through a fusion of flavors that are unabashedly different than typical restaurant flair. Unlike the massive tech startup world, food trucks are often nimble, small, and focused on a very distinct mission. They often borrow ideas from unrelated places and use ingredients that you wouldn't expect them to use.

This is what innovative teachers do all the time. They have a food truck mindset. I mentioned my friend Javi earlier in this book. Javi had a food truck mindset. When he was stuck with a rigid four-hour language block and a tight curriculum in his ELL classroom, he asked, "Why can't ELL students in a Title One school have the same kinds of projects gifted students get?"

I remember feeling frustrated by having to teach a full hour of grammar to my ELL students. Plus, I knew we would be judged on how well they did on the big ELL test at the end of the year. His response? Make the subject engaging.

When I said, "Grammar can't be fun." He laughed and asked, "Why not?"

So, I turned the constraint into a design feature and our grammar lessons became a vehicle for student blogging and podcasting projects. These were my vintage innovation lessons, combining old tools with new technology and embracing old ideas like curation and citizen journalism with newer, research-based strategies.

CONSTRAINTS

DESIGN FEATURES

I still remember a day when our district tech director came in and a student said, "Mr. Spencer, are we doing grammar today." When I said, "Not today," this girl began arguing with me. Our director's mouth dropped. Yes, this girl thought grammar was fun.

Similarly, when students struggled with volume, surface area, and proportional reasoning, I used the standards and time constraints as the building blocks on our Tiny House project. Again, we used digital tools for research and 3D modeling, but they created their houses with duct tape and cardboard. I used the Food Truck mindset I'd learned from Javi and we had one of our most successful projects of the year.

When we choose to design meaningful projects despite tight curriculum maps, limited time frames, and a lack of adequate technology, we are modeling divergent thinking for our students. Unfortunately, there's no guarantee that this will work. It might work. It could fail. And in a system focused on "best practices," this can feel risky. However, when we choose to say, "I'm going to try a different method" or "I'm going to hack the curriculum map," we end up modeling the kind of creative risk-taking we want to see in our students. The thing is, they're watching. They see the constraints we are faced with and they know when we are choosing to be divergent thinkers.

In a world of constant change, our students will need to have a food truck mindset. They will need to be nimble enough to navigate complex systems and flexible enough to handle daunting challenges. They will need to know how to experiment, iterate, and pivot as they solve multifaceted problems using limited resources. When we model risk-taking incorporate divergent thinking it into our lessons, we create the learning experiences that develop the kind of divergent thinking they'll need for the rest of their lives.

YOU'RE ALREADY AN INNOVATOR

A few years ago, my daughter entered kindergarten. She came in knowing letters but that was about it. By the end of the year, she could put together entire words. She viewed language as a playground and reading as a chance to explore a whole world. I don't completely understand the science of blending and phonics and sight words. But you do. Miraculously, millions of students learn to read every day.

Because of a teacher.

Right now, there's a teacher thinking about his students. He's dreaming of ways to make them feel safe and welcome so that they can take creative risks. For a few kids, this is the only place where they truly feel safe. His first-graders will be bold and curious in their vintage innovation makerspace. They'll become makers and divergent thinkers. They'll observe an entirely new world in the garden that he'll be planting with the rest of the first-grade teachers. They will be different . . .

Because of a teacher.

There's a language arts teacher who has taken a full week of her lunch period – those blessed 26 minutes to scarf down a meal – in order to help a student work learn how to do research. And although the progress is slow, he will become a reader and a curator and a philosopher. He'll be curious and confident as he crafts his first journalism piece. This will happen . . .

Because of a teacher.

There's a math teacher who has a room full of kids started the year saying that they're "just not good at math." But now they are geeking out over ways to solve complex problems. They are learning that math can be creative and even fun. They are chasing their curiosity, using a blend of hands-on manipulatives and high-tech gadgetry. And they will become problem-solvers.

Because of a teacher.

There's a science teacher who inspires her students to chase after their questions and on one afternoon they are so excited about their experiments that they don't even notice the bell ring. They will become scientists and experimenters.

Because of a teacher.

There is a history teacher who inspire students to capture history by filming local documentaries. Her students are already citizen journalists. There's a group of PE teachers who will encourage kids to get more active and think about their health through empathy-driven design projects. There are technology teachers who will help kids send their work to the world and fine arts teachers who help kids find their creative voice. There are foreign language teachers who are helping kids communicate globally by connecting to the local community. There are CTE teachers whose students are engaged in deep work, finally feeling like they have a place where they can succeed. They're embracing the vintage idea of "vocation," as *vocare,* a life-long calling and passion while preparing students for the jobs of the future.

IN THE END,
APPS CHANGE.
GADGETS BREAK.
TECHNOLOGY GROWS OBSOLETE.

BUT TEACHERS WILL ALWAYS
CHANGE THE WORLD.

There's a special education teacher inspiring her students to do things that once seemed impossible. She's building partnerships with the families out of a belief that all children can learn. They're doing Socratic Seminars and debating big ideas in philosophy. And there's this teacher librarian who views students as children and not data. He's creating a makerspace while also inspiring kids to fall in love with reading. They are more imaginative than ever before. They will become life-long learners . . .

Because of a teacher.

Right now, there's a 4th-grade teacher with a scribbled up yellow legal pad. She's dreaming up wild new projects and taking big creative risks. This is her 27th year and she's still innovating. To her, it's no big deal. It's what she does. But it's a big deal to her students. To them, she is a hero. This year, she is making her students' world epic, like she always does. They will remember her forever and she will change the world in ways that she cannot even fathom. And all of this will happen . . .

Because of a teacher.

Apps change. Gadgets break. Technology grows obsolete. But teachers will continue to take creative risks and experiment with new ideas. They will continue to build relationships and inspire new possibilities in their students. When our tools have grown obsolete, teachers will continue to impact lives and change the world.

REFERENCES

The following are all of the citations throughout the entire book.

[1] https://gayprideapparel.com/pages/about-us

[2] Tetlock, P. E. (2017). *Expert Political Judgment: How Good Is It? How Can We Know?- New Edition*. Princeton: Princeton University Press.

[3] Ungar, L., Mellers, B., Satopää, V., Tetlock, P., & Baron, J. (2012, October). The Good Judgment Project: A large scale test of different methods of combining expert predictions. In *2012 AAAI Fall Symposium Series*.

[4] Mellers, B., Stone, E., Atanasov, P., Rohrbaugh, N., Metz, S. E., Ungar, L., & Tetlock, P. (2015). The psychology of intelligence analysis: Drivers of prediction accuracy in world politics. *Journal of Experimental Psychology: Applied, 21*(1), 1.

[5] Tetlock, P. E., Mellers, B. A., Rohrbaugh, N., & Chen, E. (2014). Forecasting tournaments: Tools for increasing transparency and improving the quality of debate. *Current Directions in Psychological Science, 23*(4), 290-295.

[6] *Epstein, D. (2019, June). The peculiar blindness of experts. The Atlantic. Retrieved at* https://www.theatlantic.com/magazine/archive/2019/06/how-to-predict-the-future/588040/

[7] Note that Facebook CEO and Founder Mark Zuckerberg and his wife, Priscilla Chan, have invested millions in adaptive learning platforms:
Sweetland Edwards, H. (2015, December 5). Why Mark Zuckerberg wants to spend on personalized learning. *Time Magazine*. Retrieved at https://time.com/4132619/mark-zuckerberg-personalized-learning/

[8] Walker, T. (2017, June). As More Schools Look to Personalized Learning, Teaching May Be About to Change. *NEA Today*. Retrieved from http://neatoday.org/2017/06/09/personalized-learning/

[9] I know, I know. It doesn't sound true, right? However, blowing on your cartridge does more harm than good. Check out the explanation here:
Soper, T. (2014, July 2). Myth debunk: blowing in your Nintendo games never actually did anything. *GeekWire*. Retrieved at: https://www.geekwire.com/2014/blow-nintendo-games/

[10] A few pieces address the role of "filter bubbles" on ideological development.
Spohr, D. (2017). Fake news and ideological polarization: Filter bubbles and selective exposure on social media. *Business Information Review, 34*(3), 150-160.
Flaxman, S., Goel, S., & Rao, J. M. (2016). Filter bubbles, echo chambers, and online news consumption. *Public opinion quarterly, 80*(S1), 298-320.

[11] Autor, D.H. (2015). Why are there still so many jobs? The history and future of workplace automation. *Journal of Economic Perspectives, 29*(3), 3-30.

[12] Arel, I., Rose, D. C., & Karnowski, T. P. (2010). Deep machine learning-a new frontier in artificial intelligence research. *IEEE computational intelligence magazine, 5*(4), 13-18.

[13] For a deeper analysis of the relationship between AI and human analysis see: Jarrahi, M. H. (2018). Artificial intelligence and the future of work: Human-AI symbiosis in organizational decision making. *Business Horizons, 61*(4), 577-586. Consider the role of actuaries, which, according to a trade publication, will face significant disruption from AI: https://ar.casact.org/actuaries-versus-artificial-intelligence-what-do-actuaries-do-what-will-they-do/

[14] Casner-Lotto, J., & Barrington, L. (2006). *Are they really ready to work? Employers' perspectives on the basic knowledge and applied skills of new entrants to the 21st century US workforce.* Partnership for 21st Century Skills. 1 Massachusetts Avenue NW Suite 700, Washington, DC 20001.

[15] Strauss, V. (2017, December 20). The surprising thing Google learned about its employees – and what it means for today's students. *The Washington Post.*

[16] Wilson, J. (1965, April). Everyone in orbit over Astrodome. *The Sporting News.* Retrieved from http://www.astrosdaily.com/history/19650409/#article

[17] Braswell, Sean (April 9, 2015). "Flashback: When Texas Opened the 8th Wonder of the World". *OZY.*

[18] Weeks, J. (2015). Turf Wars. Retrieved September 23, 2017, from https://www.chemheritage.org/distillations/magazine/turf-wars

[19] Fitzgerald, E. (Producer). In the same ballpark. *99% Invisible* [podcast]. Retrieved from https://99percentinvisible.org/episode/in-the-same-ballpark/

[20] There's a great backstory about how Eric Moss managed to save the B&O warehouse:
Byrnes, M. (2015, September 4). Meet the man who saved Camden Yards' old warehouse. *Citylab.* Retrieved from https://www.citylab.com/design/2015/09/meet-the-man-who-saved-camden-yards-old-warehouse/403489/

[21] Teachers from all around the world have been inspired by *Caine's Arcade* and the subsequent cardboard challenges launched by the imagination foundation: https://cardboardchallenge.com/about/

[22] Dewey, J. (1897) My pedagogic creed. *School Journal,* 54, 77-80."

[23] Kilpatrick, W. H. (1918). The project method. *Teachers College Record, 19*, 319-335

[24] Szczepanska, Jo. (2017, January 3). Design thinking origin story plus some of the people who made it all happen. *Medium.* Retrieved at https://medium.com/@szczpanks/design-thinking-where-it-came-from-and-the-type-of-people-who-made-it-all-happen-dc3a05411e53

[25] Much of the hype revolved around Marzano's article touting the benefits of IWBs: Marzano, R. J. (2009). Teaching with interactive whiteboards. *Educational Leadership, 67*(3), 80-82.

[26] Guilford, J. P. (1957). Creative abilities in the arts. *Psychological Review, 64*(2), 110-118. http://dx.doi.org/10.1037/h0048280

[27] There's even a design thinking model that uses divergent and convergent thinking intermittently:

Choudhary, S. (2019, February 6). Design thinking: divergence and convergence cycles. *Medium.* Retrieved from https://medium.com/@i.shubhangich/design-thinking-divergence-and-convergence-cycles-3ce7a6f27815

[28] It is impossible to demonstrate a causal relationship between divergent thinking / creativity and standardized tests. However, since the advent of NCLB, there has been a decrease in creativity scores. While this could be due to other environmental factors, it suggests the need for schools to develop divergent thinking in students.
Kim, K. H. (2011). The creativity crisis: The decrease in creative thinking scores on the Torrance Tests of Creative Thinking. *Creativity Research Journal, 23*(4), 285-295.

[29] Fillis, I., & McAuley, A. (2000). Modeling and measuring creativity at the interface. *Journal of Marketing Theory and Practice, 8*(2), 8-17.

[30] For more on the backstory of the lawnmower, checkout:
http://www.bbc.co.uk/ahistoryoftheworld/objects/NI2ZjBwpTcqYdtpXFnIzUQ

[31] Raz, G. (Producer). Dyson: James Dyson. *How I Built That.* [Podcast]. Retrieved from https://www.npr.org/2018/03/26/584331881/dyson-james-dyson

[32] Lamar, C. (2012, June 8). The 22 rules of storytelling, according to Pixar. *Gizmodo.* Retrieved from https://io9.gizmodo.com/the-22-rules-of-storytelling-according-to-pixar-5916970

[33] In the push toward being "college and career ready," many schools have emphasized college as a first choice. However, in many industrialized nations, there is a shortage of workers for high-skilled manufacturing. There's a great article about the role of trade schools and the future of work:
St. Esprit, M. (2019, March 6). The Stigma of Choosing Trade School Over College. *The Atlantic.* Retrieved from https://www.theatlantic.com/education/archive/2019/03/choosing-trade-school-over-college/584275/

[34] NASA (2017, September 25). Engineers explore origami to create folding spacecraft. *Phys.org.* Retrieved from https://phys.org/news/2017-09-explore-origami-spacecraft.html

[35] For a deeper, in-depth look at Arya's story, check out this article:
Henry, J. (2017, October 24). How the ancient art of origami is inspiring NASA's new technologies. *Pasadena Star News.* Retrieved from https://www.pasadenastarnews.com/2017/10/04/how-the-ancient-art-of-origami-is-inspiring-nasas-new-technologies/

[36] NASA (2017, September 27). What looks good on paper may look good in space. *NASA Jet Propulsion Laboratory, California Institute of Technology.* Retrieved from: https://www.jpl.nasa.gov/news/news.php?feature=6950

[37] Coerr, E. (2004). *Sadako and the thousand paper cranes.* New York: Penguin.

[38] Bessen, J. E. (2016). How computer automation affects occupations: Technology, jobs, and skills. *Boston University School of Law: Law and Economics Research Paper,* (15-49).

[39] This is all part of a process called "probabilistic modeling" explored in this article:
Ghahramani, Z. (2015). Probabilistic machine learning and artificial intelligence. *Nature, 521*(7553), 452.

[40] Lou, N. & Peek, K. (2016, February 23). By the numbers: The rise of the makerspace. *Popular Science.* Retrieved from https://www.popsci.com/rise-makerspace-by-numbers/

[41] For an exploration of this, check out this review from the Exploratorium: https://www.exploratorium.edu/tinkering/

[42] The American Psychological Association recommends placing limitations (but not banning) high tech inputs: https://www.apa.org/helpcenter/digital-guidelines

[43] Mueller, P. A., & Oppenheimer, D. M. (2014). The pen is mightier than the keyboard: Advantages of longhand over laptop note taking. *Psychological Science, 25*(6), 1159-1168.

[44] Kelly, C. A. (2006). Using manipulatives in mathematical problem solving: A performance-based analysis. *The Mathematics Enthusiast, 3*(2), 184-193.

[45] This is a famous thought experiment in philosophy:

Judith Jarvis Thomson, *Killing, Letting Die, and the Trolley Problem*, 59 The Monist 204-17 (1976)

Judith Jarvis Thomson, "The Trolley Problem", 94 *Yale Law Journal* 1395–1415 (1985)

Francis Myrna Kamm, "Harming Some to Save Others", 57 *Philosophical Studies* 227-60 (1989)

[46] Anders, G. (2015, August 27). That 'useless' liberal arts degree has become tech's hottest ticket. *Forbes.*

[47] Fung, B. (2015, August 25). Technology companies are hiring more liberal arts majors than you think. *The Washington Post.*

[48] Segren, E. (2014, August 28). Why top tech CEOs want employees with liberal arts degrees. *Fast Company.*
Retrieved from https://www.fastcompany.com/3034947/why-top-tech-ceos-want-employees-with-liberal-arts-degrees

[49] Gregoire, C. (2017, December 6). Why philosophy majors are changing the world of business. *The Huffington Post.* Retrieved from https://www.huffpost.com/entry/why-philosophy-majors-rule_n_4891404

[50] Ha, A. (2011, May 14). Google's in-house philosopher: Technologists need a "moral operating system" *Venture Beat.*
Retrieved from https://venturebeat.com/2011/05/14/damon-horowitz-moral-operating-system/

[51] Bowles, N. (2019, March 26). Why is Silicon Valley so obsessed with the virtue of suffering? *The New York Times.* Retrieved from https://www.nytimes.com/2019/03/26/style/silicon-valley-stoics.html.

[52] Tabaka, M. (2017, December 16). Tim Ferriss says that goal-setting is important, but fear-setting is critical to success. *Inc.* Retrieved from https://www.inc.com/marla-tabaka/tim-ferris-says-you-need-this-superpower-to-achieve-mental-toughness-in-fact-it-saved-his-life.html

[53] Piper, K. (2019, February 14). An AI helped us 'write' this article. *Vox.* Retrieved from https://www.vox.com/future-perfect/2019/2/14/18222270/artificial-intelligence-open-ai-natural-language-processing

[54] Bozdag, E. (2013). Bias in algorithmic filtering and personalization. *Ethics and information technology, 15*(3), 209-227.

55 For a more nuanced idea, this article explores the notion that tech doesn't cause so much as enable narcissistic behavior:
Twenge, J. (2013, September 24). Social media is a narcissism enabler. *The New York Times*. Retrieved from https://www.nytimes.com/roomfordebate/2013/09/23/facebook-and-narcissism/social-media-is-a-narcissism-enabler

56 This is from the ground-breaking book:
Lakoff, G., & Johnson, M. (1980). *Metaphors we live by*. Chicago: University of Chicago Press.

57 Abbott, B. P., Abbott, R., Abbott, T. D., Abernathy, M. R., Acernese, F., Ackley, K., Zweizig, J. (2016). Observation of Gravitational Waves from a Binary Black Hole Merger. *Physical Review Letters*, 116(6), 61102. https://doi.org/10.1103/PhysRevLett.116.061102.

58 Hoon Yao Tong, R., & Chiew Pheng, P. (2009). Metaphorical conceptions of min in Pre-Qin Confucian mind-nature discourses. Singapore: *Proceedings of the URECA@Nanyang Technical Institute*. Retrieved from http://www.academia.edu/602658/Metaphorical_Conceptions_of_MIND_in_Pre-Qin_Confucian_Mind-Nature_Discourses

59 Epstein, R. (2016, May). Your brain does not process information and it is not a computer. *Aeon*.
Retrieved from https://aeon.co/essays/your-brain-does-not-process-information-and-it-is-not-a-computer.

60 McCoy, A. N., & Tan, S. Y. (2014). Otto Loewi (1873-1961): Dreamer and Nobel laureate.
Singapore Medical Journal, 55(1), 3–4. https://doi.org/10.11622/SMEDJ.2014002

61 Plato. (1921). *Theaetetus*. (H.N. Fowler, Tran.) London: W. Heinemann.

62 For a great demonstration of this check out:
https://www.youtube.com/watch?list=PLIFDiU2PVB8DQ1Qf7cGNvRV2HSMOWUBMf&v=Y3ROyorFv5E

63 You can find more information here: http://www.weareastepahead.com/community/doll-prosthetics/

64 Online Etymology Dictionary: https://www.etymonline.com/word/compassion

65 Thomas, S. (2018, March 4). Empathy vs. "Compassion" (aka "Dangerous Minds etc.). *Medium*. Retrieved from https://medium.com/sarahdateechur/empathy-vs-compassion-aka-dangerous-minds-et-7019b331d9be

66 https://dschool.stanford.edu/

67 Brown, T., & Katz, B. (2011). Change by design. *Journal of Product Innovation Management*, 28(3), 381-383.

68 Spencer, J. & Juliani, A. J. (2016). *Launch: Using design thinking to boost creativity and bring out the maker in every student*. Dave Burgess Consulting, Incorporated.

69 Vilson, J. (2013, February 21). Empowering students through empathy and collaboration. *Edutopia*. Retrieved from https://www.edutopia.org/blog/empowering-students-empathy-collaboration-jose-vilson

70 Wineburg, S., McGrew, S., Breakstone, J., & Ortega, T. (2016). Evaluating information: The cornerstone of civic online reasoning. *Stanford Digital Repository*. *Retrieved January, 8*, 2018.

[71] http://sugarkills.us/

[72] Wall, M. (2015). Citizen journalism. *Digital Journalism*. 3(6). 797-813.

[73] Hughes, W. (2011). Citizen Journalism: Historical roots and contemporary challenges. *Western Kentucky Thesis:*
https://digitalcommons.wku.edu/cgi/viewcontent.cgi?article=1311&context=stu_hon_theses

[74] Muir, T. (2017). *The Epic Classroom: How to Boost Engagement, Make Learning Memorable, and Transform Lives.* Salem: Blend Education.

[75] While cultural humility is a term most closely associated with the healthcare industry, there are many implications for students and teachers as well.
Tervalon, M., & Murray-Garcia, J. (1998). Cultural humility versus cultural competence: A critical distinction in defining physician training outcomes in multicultural education. *Journal of health care for the poor and underserved, 9*(2), 117-125.

[76] Janet Eyler is known as one of the founders of the service learning movement. She co-wrote a great piece here:
Eyler, J., & Giles Jr, D. E. (1999). *Where's the Learning in Service-Learning? Jossey-Bass Higher and Adult Education Series.* Jossey-Bass, Inc., 350 Sansome St., San Francisco, CA 94104.
If you're interested in the connection between service learning, social justice, and multicultural competence, check out this article:
Einfeld, A., & Collins, D. (2008). The relationships between service-learning, social justice, multicultural competence, and civic engagement. *Journal of College Student Development, 49*(2), 95-109.

[77] Waukee Community School District. Russ Goerend Presented the ITEC Outstanding Educator Award. Retrieved from https://waukeeschools.org/news/2016/10/russ-goerend-presented-the-itec-outstanding-educator-award/

[78] Oppezzo, M., & Schwartz, D. L. (2014). Give your ideas some legs: The positive effect of walking on creative thinking. *Journal of experimental psychology: learning, memory, and cognition, 40*(4), 1142.

[79] Soojung-Kim Pang, A. (2016) Rest: *Why You Get More Done When You Work Less.* New York: Basic Books.

[80] Marselle, M. R., Irvine, K. N., & Warber, S. L. (2014). Examining group walks in nature and multiple aspects of well-being: A large-scale study. *Ecopsychology, 6*(3), 134-147.

[81] Boesel, L. F., Greiner, C., Arzt, E., & Del Campo, A. (2010). Gecko-inspired surfaces: a path to strong and reversible dry adhesives. *Advanced Materials, 22*(19), 2125-2137.

[82] Jiang, H., Hawkes, E. W., Fuller, C., Estrada, M. A., Suresh, S. A., Abcouwer, N., ... & Cutkosky, M. R. (2017). A robotic device using gecko-inspired adhesives can grasp and manipulate large objects in microgravity. *Science Robotics, 2*(7), eaan4545.

[83] Egerton, F. N. (2006). A history of the ecological sciences, part 21: Réaumur and his history of insects.

[84] Sawai, H. (2012, June). Reorganizing a new generation airline network based on an ant-colony optimization-inspired small-world network. In *2012 IEEE Congress on Evolutionary Computation* (pp. 1-8). IEEE.

[85] Many of the ideas are explored in this article:

Rowley, T. (2013). Science imitates life. *Lab animal, 42*(8), 271.

[86] Snell-Rood, E. (2016). Interdisciplinarity: Bring biologists into biomimetics. *Nature News, 529*(7586), 277.

[87] Benyus, J. M. (1997). *Biomimicry: Innovation Inspired By Nature.* New York: Perennial.

[88] Manu, A. (2006). *The Imagination Challenge: Strategic Foresight And Innovation In The Global Economy.* New Riders.

[89] Tabaka, M. (2015, October 12). How video games can train your brain to be more creative and productive. *Inc.* Retrieved from https://www.inc.com/marla-tabaka/how-video-games-can-train-your-brain-to-be-more-creative-and-productive.html

[90] Greenfield, P. M. (2009). Technology and informal education: What is taught, what is learned. *Science, 323*(5910), 69-71.

[91] Land, G., & Jarman, B. (1993). *Breakpoint and Beyond: Mastering The Future--Today.* HarperCollins.

[92] Lieberman, J. N. (1965). Playfulness and divergent thinking: An investigation of their relationship at the kindergarten level. *The Journal of Genetic Psychology, 107*(2), 219-224.

[93] Costikyan, G. (2005). Game styles, innovation, and new audiences: An historical view. Simon Fraser University.

[94] Costikyan, G. (2013). *Uncertainty in Games.* Cambridge: Mit Press.

[95] Schlechty, P. C. (2011). *Engaging students: The next level of working on the work.* New York: John Wiley & Sons.

[96] There's also evidence that they can hit a state of Flow in collaborative games: Admiraal, W., Huizenga, J., Akkerman, S., & Ten Dam, G. (2011). The concept of flow in collaborative game-based learning. *Computers in Human Behavior, 27*(3), 1185-1194.

[97] Devonshire, I. M., Davis, J., Fairweather, S., Highfield, L., Thaker, C., Walsh, A., ... & Hathway, G. J. (2014). Risk-based learning games improve long-term retention of information among school pupils. *PloS one, 9*(7), e103640.

[98] For a sense of what this process looks like check out:

Pivec, M., Dziabenko, O., & Schinnerl, I. (2003, July). Aspects of game-based learning. In *3rd International Conference on Knowledge Management, Graz, Austria* (pp. 216-225).

[99] Beaudin, L., & Ratther, O. (2019, July). Game play: Fostering empathy through game-based learning. In *Global Learn* (pp. 154-161). Association for the Advancement of Computing in Education (AACE).

[100] For a primer on visible thinking strategies check out:

Ritchhart, R., & Perkins, D. (2008). Making thinking visible. *Educational leadership, 65*(5), 57.

Also, check out this book:

Ritchhart, R., Church, M., & Morrison, K. (2011). *Making Thinking Visible: How To Promote Engagement, Understanding, And Independence For All Learners.* New York: John Wiley & Sons.

[101] Allen, P. (2016, November 14). If you want to be a writer, Neil Gaiman says you should "get bored." *LifeHacker*. Retrieved on https://lifehacker.com/if-you-want-to-be-a-writer-neil-gaiman-says-you-should-1788961635

[102] Lewis, M. (2016). *The Undoing Project: A Friendship That Changed The World*. London: Penguin UK.

[103] Newport, C. (2016). *Deep work: Rules for focused success in a distracted world*. New York: Grand Central Publishing.

[104] Nakamura, J., & Csikszentmihalyi, M. (2009). Flow theory and research. *Handbook Of Positive Psychology*, 195-206.

[105] Csikszentmihalyi, M. (1997). *Finding Flow: The Psychology Of Engagement With Everyday Life*. New York: Basic Books

[106] Czikszentmihalyi, M. (1990). *Flow: The Psychology Of Optimal Experience*. New York: Harper & Row.

[107] Jones, B. F., Rasmussen, C. M., & Moffitt, M. C. (1997). Real-life problem solving.: A collaborative approach to interdisciplinary learning. Washington, DC: American Psychological Association.

[108] Thomas, J. W. & Mergendoller, J. R. (2000). Managing project-based learning: Principles from the field. Paper presented at the Annual Meeting of the American Educational Research Association, New Orleans.

[109] Parkinson, C.N. (1955, November 19). Parkinson's Law. *The Economist*.

[110] Spencer, J., & Juliani, A. J. (2016). *Launch: Using Design Thinking To Boost Creativity And Bring Out The Maker In Every Student*. Dave Burgess Consulting, Incorporated.

111 This idea is explored in this podcast episode: Malone, K., Gonzalez, S., & Horowitz-Ghazi, A. "Episode 877: The Laws Of The Office" [podcast] Planet Money. Retrieved from https://www.npr.org/sections/money/2018/11/19/669395064/episode-877-the-laws-of-the-office

[112] Chambers, D. W., & Glassman, P. (1997). A primer on competency-based evaluation. *Journal of Dental Education, 61*(8), 651-66.

[113] Hattie explains this in-depth in the following video: https://www.youtube.com/watch?v=YUooOYbgSUg

[114] Murphy Paul, A. (2013, March). Why feeling confused will help you learn better. Retrieved from http://anniemurphypaul.com/2013/02/why-feeling-confused-will-help-you-learn-better/

[115] Muller, D. A., Sharma, M. D., Eklund, J., & Reimann, P. (2007). Conceptual change through vicarious learning in an authentic physics setting. *Instructional Science, 35*(6), 519-533. See also: https://teachingcommons.stanford.edu/teaching-talk/when-confusing-lecture-better-clear-lecture

[116] Pedaste, M., Mäeots, M., Siiman, L. A., De Jong, T., Van Riesen, S. A., Kamp, E. T., ... & Tsourlidaki, E. (2015). Phases of inquiry-based learning: Definitions and the inquiry cycle. *Educational Research Review, 14*, 47-61.

[117] Banchi, H., & Bell, R. (2008). The many levels of inquiry. *Science And Children, 46*(2), 26.

[118] Meyer, D. (2010). Math class needs a makeover. *TED talks*.

[119] Taken from the Online Etymology Dictionary: https://www.etymonline.com/word/curate

[120] Morton, T. (2011, September 9). A brief history of the word 'curator.' *Phaidon.* Retrieved from https://www.phaidon.com/agenda/art/articles/2011/september/09/a-brief-history-of-the-word-curator/

[121] There's a great exploration of why curation is a necessary digital competency here:
Cohen, M. A., James, N., & Mihailidis, P. (2013). Exploring curation as a core competency in digital and media literacy education.

[122] Jameson, A. B. (1877). *A Commonplace Book Of Thoughts, Memories And Fancies, Original And Selected.*

ABOUT THE
AUTHOR

JOHN SPENCER

John Spencer a former middle school teacher and current college professor on a on a mission to see teachers unleash the creative potential in all of their students. He regularly explores research, interviews educators, deconstructs systems, and studies real-world examples of design thinking in action. He shares these insights in books, blog posts, journal articles, free resources, animated videos, and podcasts.

In Spencer's second year of teaching, he used design thinking for a student-centered documentary project. He spent the next decade on a journey to empower his students to become creative thinkers and problem-solvers. This meant mural projects, service learning projects, designing STEM camps, and creating coding projects.

Along the way, he helped develop the student-friendly LAUNCH Cycle, a design thinking framework for K-12 students. He is the co-author of the bestselling books Launch and Empower. In 2013, he spoke at the White House, sharing a vision for how to empower students to be future-ready through creativity and design thinking. John Spencer has led workshops and delivered keynotes around the world.

BRING JOHN SPENCER TO YOUR SCHOOL OR EVENT

John Spencer is passionate about seeing educators embrace design thinking and creativity. Over the last few years, he has shared this vision for creative classroom with a variety of audiences, including his speech in the White House about the future of education and his TEDx Talk on creativity.

John offers a creative, thought-provoking, and humorous style through his keynotes, full-day workshops and online professional development. He offers the unique perspective of being a published author, the co-founder of a successful startup, an award-winning classroom teacher, and a college professor. He uses this blend of classroom experience, industry experience, and research experience to craft innovative, holistic, and practical learning experiences in a style that is approachable and relevant.

Check it out at: http://www.spencerauthor.com/speaking-and-consulting/

Connect
Connect with John Spencer for more information about bringing him to your event.

Email: john@spencerauthor.com
Twitter: @spencerideas
Blog: spencerauthor.com
YouTube: spencervideos.com and videoprompts.com

CPSIA information can be obtained
at www.ICGtesting.com
Printed in the USA
LVHW030004130120
643403LV00015B/1366/P